BOONE COUNTY LIBRARY

2040 9100 315 004 3

WITHDRAWN

BOONE COUNTY PUBLIC LIBRARY
8899 U.S. 42
UNION, KY 41091

JUL 0 9 2003

# Handbags

# Handbags

## A PEEK INSIDE A WOMAN'S MOST TRUSTED ACCESSORY

by BARBARA G. S. HAGERTY

Foreword by Anne Rivers Siddons

## RUNNING PRESS

PHILADELPHIA · LONDON

© 2002 by Barbara G. S. Hagerty
Foreword © 2002 by Anne Rivers Siddons
All rights reserved under the Pan-American and International Copyright Conventions
Printed in China

*This book may not be reproduced in whole or in part, in any form or by any means, electronic or mechanical, including photocopying, recording, or by any information storage and retrieval system now known or hereafter invented, without written permission from the publisher.*

9  8  7  6  5  4  3  2  1
Digit on the right indicates the number of this printing

Library of Congress Cataloging-in-Publication Number 2002100476

ISBN 0-7624-1330-1

Cover and interior photography © Jack Alterman
Cover and interior design by Alicia Freile
Edited by Melissa Wagner
Typography: Sabon, Futura, and Coronet

This book may be ordered by mail from the publisher.
Please include $2.50 for postage and handling.
*But try your bookstore first!*

Running Press Book Publishers
125 South Twenty-second Street
Philadelphia, Pennsylvania 19103-4399

Visit us on the web!
www.runningpress.com

Editor's Note: Every effort has been made to identify old handbags and give proper accreditation, but in some instances we were not able to do so because the name of the manufacturer/designer is not known. We apologize for any inconvenience.

to A.M.S. and M.L.H.
and to my husband, R.C.H.,
still baffled by handbags

# TABLE OF CONTENTS

# *Foreword*

Aside from shoes (and wouldn't Freud have a good time with that), purses are the article of dress that inspire the strongest emotions in women, from the mythical Diana on down to the modern woman who carries her Manolo Blahniks to the office in a Fendi tote. Love, mistrust, jealousy, playfulness, hauteur, primal femininity—they're all there in our relationship with the bags we carry with us, and they always have been.

Sir James George Frazer, in his seminal and dizzying study of myth and magic, *The Golden Bough,* tells of Diana, who carried a pouch for her game and her arrows. The Delphic Oracles kept the substances they burned to enter their trance states in bags tied to their wrists. The chatelaines of the castles of the Middle Ages had girdle pouches in which household necessities were kept. The Santeria priests and priestesses of the Caribbean kept their obeahs, or charms, in a neck pouch. Women of the last century kept their fancy work in bags that went everywhere with them. Today's young women carry a small pouch just large enough for keys, driver's license, and credit card.

Jung thought that the purse, or pouch, was the archetypal symbol for the fertile, secret womb and, as such, largely the province of women. Surely, the nattily black-dressed young men you see scurrying about the streets of New York with their shoulder bags do not invest them with the sheer power that women do their purses.

For purses are about power. Utility and status aside, they are an outward symbol of what most empowers their owners, and they can reflect the various power personas of any one woman at different times. A woman has no need to wear her heart on her sleeve. To the astute observer, she is showing you who she is every time she takes her purse out her door.

Consider this: My mother (and maybe yours) believed her power was invested in ladyhood—in a sweet stew of correctness, kindness, utility, and unobtrusiveness. Thus the square, double-handled leather pocketbook that dangled from her arm wherever she went. In it was a lace hankie smelling of gardenias, a pair of small scissors, her pink lipstick, enough money to call a taxi or lend to someone in an emergency, LifeSavers to soothe children and prevent offense with the breath, and her department store credit cards. The purse itself would be substantial and gracefully formed, but its leather would invariably be black, navy, or brown, with a madcap fling into white after Easter and before Labor Day. Mother was a Lady. So was Princess Grace. That was their power.

Or the woman, like me, whose capacious, clanking bag harbors everything from the essential money, credit cards, and driver's license to screwdrivers, dried-up ballpoints, wadded-up sales receipts, unused saccharine tablets from years back, a paperback book in case I have to wait someplace, half of a pack of cheese crackers, and packets of flea repellent for the cats. I think that my power must lie in the fact that I have everything with me to sustain life for a decent length of time. Carelessness, readiness, a certain willingness to be thought unfashionable—I think those things empower me. I think they do a lot of women who live out of their purses.

The clutch purse—the tiny, pretty, hideously expensive ones you see carried in manicured hands at such American royal pageants as the Academy Awards—say: "My power is that I am complete. I am beautiful, admired, infinitely desirable. I need nothing to adorn or finish me except this scrap of satin and crystal that holds my house key, so I can lock the intruding world out." This is the power of hauteur, and it is seductive and great fun. I get a whiff of it whenever I carry a little black satin clutch. I'll bet we all do.

The shoulder bag says that there is power in the freedom it affords, in the cheeky exuberance of its dash and swing. Free-spiritedness—a strong and empowering persona.

The novelty bag, the purse that is strictly for fun and show, is a light-hearted statement: "Let me entertain you. I am confident enough that I do not need correctness. I would like to make you happy when you look at my purse. This is a side of me I give you like a gift." Pure, potent power—the power of play.

The purse with the maker's initials all over it? Power certainly, even if borrowed. This is maybe the most poignant power of all: on the days when you feel bled of all power and freedom, smacked in the face by the sheer fact of living in the world, the Chanel or Yves St. Laurent or Gucci purse you saved for a year to buy goes a long way in restoring you back to the ranks of the powerful and formidable. It is sometimes fashionable to deride the "initial purse," but there are an awful lot of us who reach for it like a Band-Aid. I have a Chanel bag I bought with my first royalty check. I still feel, by God, like a woman of substance when I go out with it.

Barbara Hagerty has caught all these powers and piquancies in this charming and provocative book. You will meet women to whom their handbags are literally their identities. To whom they are reservoirs of privacy and secrets—and who hasn't gotten annoyed at the husband or child or friend who rummages unbidden through our purses? Women to whom they are symbols of luxury and status, of memory and nostalgia, of pure fun and fantasy. Women who, like Virginia Parker of Atlanta, see their purses as "a cave that contains the map to my life—what I'm currently interested in, responsible for, creating."

These women are all of us, and any of us, and in their ranks you will find enough power to light the world up for a good year or two. Enjoy it. Power to the purses!

—Anne Rivers Siddons
February 14, 2002

# *Preface*

## "One's handbag is an extension of self, persona, personality . . ."

—Leila Hadley Luce
Writer and former cartoon editor, *The Saturday Evening Post*

The genesis of *Handbags* stretches back to childhood, when I first began to observe my mother's handbag and its importance in her life. Intuitively, I equated that handbag with womanhood and all its attendant powers and mysteries. As a daydreaming little girl, I believed that to possess such a handbag would be to cross, *as in a fairy tale,* over a magical threshold into female adulthood and become initiated into a world of womanly privileges and responsibilities.

I remember my mother's rigid, short-handled, ladylike "pocketbook" which she—in dress, pearls, nylon stockings, and high heels—carried from Junior League meeting to bridge table to church. Mysterious, feminine, possessed of a dark, hidden interior, Mother's pocketbook was a little cosmos of its own. And it was off-limits, as well. I never went into it without asking permission. A request to rummage through that inner sanctum for peppermints or dimes was met with sidelong glances and caveats: not to displace anything; not to rearrange anything; and—anxiety of anxieties—not to lose the bag itself. Clearly, her handbag was more than a container for necessities. It held meanings having to do with identity, privacy, security, and serenity. These meanings became even clearer as I matured and began to carry—and rely upon—a handbag of my own.

Over the years, my interest in feminine culture and psychology grew, and I wrote often on themes pertinent to women. I am also a poet with an interest in symbol, metaphor, and the numinous object: the animate, supernatural, even spiritual quality of so-called ordinary, inanimate, everyday things. About four years ago I brought these interests together by writing two columns for *Skirt!* magazine, in which I began to explore the highly connotative and richly paradoxical nature of purses. Purses are both physical and metaphysical, practical and poetic, universal and unique. They are icon, totem, fetish. They echo female anatomy in their essentially female shape. They suggest womb, heart, breast, and psyche. They are worn or carried in the body's most intimate zone. They are a small extension of the self that goes forth into the world while maintaining an utterly private dimension.

Thus began an adventure which is now in its fifth year and has taken me on guided tours through the handbags, closets, hearts, and minds of hundreds of women all over the United States. After publishing the columns, I realized I had only begun to explore the topic and thus began what I called "The Purse Project," an adventure documenting purses and their owners with my camera, ultimately creating a gallery of sixty-five black-and-white 35 mm portraits. I also interviewed each purse owner at length, later editing these narratives down to their essence and eventually exhibiting and publishing them alongside the photographs. As I spoke to women in the course of the project, I sometimes felt as though I had unloosed a floodgate. Stories came in torrents. Memories bubbled to the surface. Eyes misted over as women showed me the tattered, well-loved handbags that had once belonged to their grandmothers.

Although the history of the handbag has been well-documented by fashion historians—and its significance as a symbol of power, energy, and identity is well known to psychoanalysts and artists—little if anything has been written from the point-of-view of the handbag owners themselves.

Exploring the central idea that the purse is an extension of persona, The "Purse Project" gathered momentum, ultimately resulting in four visual arts exhibits (one each in New York and Washington, and two in Charleston) and a book (*Purse Universe*, Crane Hill Publishers, 2001). Along the way, the work was awarded an Annual Artist's grant by the South Carolina Arts Commission (which is supported by the National Endowment for the Arts) in 1999. As awareness of my work grew, I became known as "the bag lady" and people approached me with stories, memories, and what I call "purse theories"—why a bag must be one way or another, or have a particular physical, or metaphysical, quality.

At this juncture, I recognized that in addition to their symbolic properties, handbags harbor and project important themes, such as identity, privacy, power, status, security, luxury, dreams, and more. That realization is the basis for this book. *Handbags* identifies and deconstructs these themes, looking beneath and beyond fashion into the fetishism of the purse, the deep attachments and the astounding power such a quotidian object has to arouse in its owner memory, emotion, message, or meaning.

Above all it is a Valentine, a celebration of the most quintessentially feminine of belongings. It is a brainchild born of equal parts seriousness, curiosity, joy, and affection. Best of all, it was put together by a loose sisterhood of women, for this is the sort of project that could never be accomplished by one woman alone, but rather depends on the myriad perceptions of many. I put the word "out there" by letter and e-mail to women around the country—writers, artists, stay-at-home moms, grandmothers, professional women, students, and more—inviting handbag commentary, histories, theories, memories, and anecdotes. I was greatly rewarded—not only by the volume of replies, many from total strangers, but also by their insightfulness, warmth, openness, and generosity.

# Acknowledgments

Though just one person is listed as author, *Handbags* is a collaboration among friends—new friends, old friends, nearby friends, far flung friends, and friends I've never met. You told me your stories, wrote down your memories, and entrusted me with your handbags. Handbags wrapped in acid-free tissue, stored in hatboxes, or tucked away at the back of a lingerie drawer. Handbags unearthed from attic trunks, or mailed across the country, or whisked from the security of a bank vault. Pedigreed bags. Funky bags. Artistic bags. Original bags. Loved like treasures, revered like reliquaries, and pondered like the holograms they are.

One of the hazards of knowing writers is that they tend to envelop you in their obsessions. Each woman who helped in the collaboration is special, but a few must be named individually for entering deeply into my passion for the poetics and aesthetics of pocketbooks: Kelly Chambers, for research and artistry, Lori Wyatt, Barbara Julius, Judith Green, Cada McCoy, Bessie Hanahan, Harriett Daughtridge, Carlene Sessions, Tippy Brickman, Sonya Livingston, Deb Moissinac, Mary Douglas, Jane McFadden, Peggy Lewis, Sandi Mohlmann, Gretchen Freeman, Ellen Rachlin, and the people at Oroton and MooRoo.

Warm appreciation goes to Anne Rivers Siddons for over twenty years of generous friendship; Ginger Barber, a muse over the onset of this project; Larry Ashmead, for his inimitable Rolodex; and to a few good men: Tom Blagden, Rich Halperin, and especially Jack Alterman for his stunning photography.

Thanks also go to the editors at Running Press, Melissa Wagner and Jennifer Worick, who shared my vision for this book from the first day forward, and to the book's graphic designer, Ali Freile, whose love of beauty and whimsy shows on every page.

Finally, and with love, I thank my family: two Richards, Gervais, Curry, and Hart, who accompanied me on this four-year-long Penelopeaid through the metaphysics of purses. My life has been rich in family and friends. You are the best.

# Introduction

The world is full of objects that have value, utility, and meaning. For a woman, the most essential of these is her handbag.

Although she may cherish her wedding ring and honor her country's flag, her handbag is the one item without which she can't function. Of all her belongings—and by whatever name it's called, whether *handbag, bag, purse,* or old-fashioned *pocketbook*—this quintessential feminine object is not only the most indispensable but also the most symbolically-charged and the best-loved.

Women's love affair with handbags has never been hotter and heavier. Designers declared the end of the 1990s a "handbag moment." Fashion magazines continue to describe consumer desire at fever pitch and feature photos of models in obvious states of Handbag Lust and Purse Envy. Women, fashion writers say, are more "obsessed" than ever by the latest handbag styles, and are willing to pay top dollar or put their names on long waiting lists for them.

The facts corroborate this phenomenon. According to recent statistics in *Accessories* magazine, handbags dominated the accessories market, accounting for $4.94 billion in sales in 1999, eclipsed only by jewelry. Handbags always fit. They are relatively inexpensive. They take up little room in the closet. Classic bags never go out of style. Funky bags remain interesting. Valuable bags can be passed along to a daughter.

But fashion is only part—the least part—of the tale. The handbag is more than the sum of its parts. Mystery supercedes manner. Mind outweighs matter. Substance trumps style.

The reason is that every handbag tells a unique story. Even if the bag has been mass-produced, any one bag is carried by a single owner who, over time and in the course of her experiences, invests that bag with her individual history.

The handbag goes where she goes. It meets whom she meets. It experiences what she experiences. It's a comrade-in-arms throughout the adventures of her life.

Asking a woman about her handbag is like giving her a Rorschach test. Like the ink blot, the bag's familiar pattern is a sort of screen onto which she can project her longings, beliefs, attentions, intentions, idiosyncrasies—and anxieties. For not all women look fondly on their handbags. Some women associate them with deprivation, insecurity, or unwanted responsibilities.

But to the overwhelming majority of women they are complex objects worthy of esteem, affection, and celebration. Their kaleidoscopic contradictions and inherent paradoxes simply enrich an already complex relationship. Whether it's perceived as cultural icon, artwork, protector, companion, alter ego, or all of the above, the handbag—more than any other feminine object—represents powerful, even mythic, dimensions of the female story.

# A Short History of the Handbag

*"A dagger and a purse of woven silk*
*Hung at his girdle, white as morning milk."*

—from "The Franklin"
by Geoffrey Chaucer (1340–1400)
English writer

The history of the handbag and its antecedent and close cousin, the purse, follows the trajectory of women's liberation. In the beginning, the purse strings belonged to—who else?—*men!*

The development of the purse goes back to ancient Greek and Roman civilizations, when the need arose for a small pouch in which to carry coins. Constructed of animal hide, this coin purse was known as *byrsa* by the Greeks and *bursa* by the Romans. These terms still exist in our modern vocabulary, such as in the English words *purse* and *bursar,* or treasurer; in the French word

*This flat mesh chatelaine bag is made of German silver. The elaborate silver frame is embossed with pansies and rosebuds. It has been engraved with the date "1902."*

*Bourse,* for stock exchange; in the Italian term for purse, *borsa;* and in the Spanish, *bolsa.*

Men continued to hold onto the purse strings in the Middle Ages, wearing *almonieres,* or alms bags, when they traveled on their Crusades. These bags were hung from girdles the men wore around their waists, and contained alms to be given to poor people they encountered along their journeys eastward.

Women, of course, remained at home in charge of household or castle. Thus the feminine custom began of wearing a chatelaine, or hooklike clasp, around the waist, to which were attached small necessities such as scissors, pincushion, or keys. In time, the woman herself became known as a *chatelaine,* or mistress of the castle, another term which survives today.

The development of the pocket, beginning around the sixteenth century, permitted men and women alike the convenience of carrying objects in their clothing. Early women's pockets were attached to long ribbons, tied around the waist, and accessed via slashes in the skirt; later, the pockets were sewn into the garments. As long as women's skirts were voluminous, the added bulk of pockets was not a problem.

In the eighteenth century, however, a vogue for slender, Grecian, neoclassical dresses emerged. To keep the body's silhouette lean, women no longer wanted lumpy, bulging pockets. Thus, the first women's bags—or reticules—evolved. Often made of luxurious fabrics like velvet and silk and embellished with ribbons and tassels, reticules were dainty, petite, and ladylike.

According to fashion historian Claire Wilcox in her book *A Century of Bags*, "such bags became known as 'indispensibles' in Britain and 'ridicules' in France, and were naturally the subject of gentle humor, as befitted an item that had made the transition from private to public. As the nineteenth century progressed, the term 'ridicule' evolved into 'reticule,' a term that was used in both French and English up to 1912."

The creation of the reticule dovetailed naturally with women's mastery of the needle arts. Still largely confined to hearth and home, women lavished energy and artistry on making and embellishing their reticules. Knitting, netting, embroidering, and cross-stitching them became popular past-times that persisted into the early twentieth century.

"I was shown into a pretty . . . drawing room and there sat Agnes, netting a purse. She looked so quiet and good . . ."

—from *David Copperfield*
by Charles Dickens (1812–1870)
English novelist

Toward the conclusion of the 1800s, however, extraordinary cultural changes were in motion. The Industrial Revolution had occurred, and large numbers of women were employed in offices and factories. Suffragettes demanded women's voting rights in the United States and abroad. Travel by train and steamship became commonplace, and the advent of automobile and commercial air travel were just a few years in the future.

Around 1880, luggage makers began to manufacture a sturdy leather bag with a handle for the woman traveler. Much smaller than her luggage, it was designed to be carried in the hand—as opposed to dangled or draped from wrist or waist like her soft, fabric reticule.

When women assumed new roles outside the home—as workers, wage earners, students, and travelers—their handbags changed relatively rapidly from dainty trifles to serious objects, indeed. Nobody thought of them as *ridiculous* anymore.

*This glass-beaded purse has an imitation tortoiseshell frame and handle and was one of many beautiful objects collected by the owner's great-grandmother. In addition to attending auctions, she liked to wander through little antiques shops in the countryside where treasures like this one could be found.*

The modern handbag as we understand it evolved quickly and continuously. Its story is always unfolding, for the handbag's form constantly shifts, chameleon-like, to accommodate and reflect trends, tastes, needs, mores, and scientific developments in the larger cultural context. War and peace; depression and affluence; prohibition and indulgence—the development of bags happens against the broader social backdrop of an age.

Fashion, by definition, is dynamic; fashion *is* change. Each decade or two has brought radically new interpretations to the basic form of the bag as well as revivals or reinterpre-tations of old styles. To name but a few: the clutches and beaded or metal mesh bags of the Roaring Twenties; the military-inspired shoulder bags of the 1940s; the fun, plastic bags of the Eisenhower years; the logo-covered bags and nylon backpacks of the "designer" 1980s; the handsome tote bags of the late 1990s; and the soft, ergonomic bags—contoured and strapped to torso or hips—of today.

In short, the handbag—like the woman who carries it—has been freed from old constraints and expectations. Both have been liberated, and anything is possible!

*These three MooRoos are named, left to right, "Carmen Miranda," "Maui Wowie," and "Strut Your Stuff." One of the hottest handbag designers on the scene, MooRoo has been making bags only since 1998. Favored by celebrities, MooRoos are owned by actresses Andie MacDowell, Sharon Stone, Leeza Gibbons, and Courteney Cox-Arquette, among many others.*

# INDEED, I THOUGHT,
## SLIPPING THE SILVER INTO MY PURSE,
# IT IS REMARKABLE,
## REMEMBERING THE BITTERNESS OF THOSE DAYS,
# WHAT A CHANGE IN TEMPER
## A FIXED INCOME WILL BRING ABOUT.

—from *A Room of One's Own*
by Virginia Woolf (1882–1941)
English writer

*"Passion Flower" is from Mary Frances's
Motif Collection. With its heart shape
and rosy color, it resembles a Valentine
on a pretty chain.*

# Identity & Individuality

*King Louis* the XIV of France famously said: *"L'etat, cest moi"* ("The state is me"). Today's woman, so identified is she with her handbag, could justly make a similar claim. I am my handbag. My handbag is me. We are joined at the hip. We are a mutually dependent system. A dynamic duo. An inseparable pair, with secrets and powers between us. My handbag doesn't just belong to me: it *is* me, my alter ego.

The identity that an average handbag contains is quite literal: driver's license, social security card, health insurance card, credit cards, and sometimes a passport or birth certificate—proof that you exist, proof of who you are. Also, various PIN numbers and user ID numbers—access to bank and telecommunications—and the telephone numbers of key people such as banker, broker, astrologist, psychiatrist, insurance agent, hairdresser, doctor, acupuncturist . . . no wonder the loss of such a handbag is tantamount to losing oneself, albeit temporarily. And if it is lost, it must be replaced *immediately* so that the owner can get on with her life.

On its most basic level, the handbag is a practical container that helps its owner venture forth from home. The bag and its contents support transitions—whether brief or lengthy—through time and space.

The second most basic function of the handbag is to project—or conceal—identity. As a woman's roles in society have expanded, so have the prisms of her identity. Correspondingly, her handbags have expanded and multiplied. They are bigger in general, and she now has a wardrobe of them!

For instance, a working woman may arrive at her office in the morning carrying a roomy, important leather handbag.

For a lunch date, she whips out a smaller bag— just big enough for lipstick and credit card—which "lives" inside the main handbag. Later, she shows up at the fitness center with her gear stashed in a sporty microfiber tote. That evening, she's seen a charity fundraiser holding a fragile, gossamer evening bag.

The same woman may shift from boss to friend to gym rat to mother to healer to femme fatale all in one twenty-four-hour period, and her handbag facilitates all these metamorphoses.

*These three chic black purses were all made by Salvatore Ferragamo in the 1990s. The purse on the left with the long gold chain features a grosgrain ribbon placed across its width. The bag at center has an unusual strap shaped like a Moebius strip. At right is a diminutive purse intended to be worn as a necklace.*

The handbag is a form of autobiography, offering a snapshot of its owner, a fleeting portrait in time. And the medium could be anything. Whereas only about a hundred years ago bags were principally made of fabric or animal hide, these days the media may be unusual, or even eccentric: duct tape, Astroturf, PVC, rubber, uncooked pasta, raffia, wire, stone, aluminum, seeds, or fish vertebrae! And why not? Today's woman is not at home sewing. She's designing skyscrapers, sequencing DNA, or orbiting in space.

The contents of bags offer further clues to identity. Before 1900, a traditional drawstring bag may have held a thimble, smelling salts, and fan. A contemporary handbag may contain Mace, a collapsible umbrella, cell phone, Palm Pilot, baby's pacifier, artificial sweetener, Band-Aids, birth control, maps, jewelry, multivitamin, business cards, tea bags, bottled water, spiritual rock, safety pins, sunglasses, pantyhose, and a CD player. A woman's handbag

*Young, twenty-something artist Savannah Knoop calls this purse a "Tink" bag— "like the sound you hear when something drops." The bag has a bamboo handle attached to a pair of chains and is made of duct tape sewn with dental floss. "It's waterproof, too," she says.*

has as many identities as she does: portable office, pharmacy, museum, photo gallery, bank, church or temple, dressing room, beauty salon, cafeteria, telecommunications center, jukebox, or waste paper basket.

Understanding handbags as an extension of identity, women often consciously employ them to enhance—or decrease—individuality, to make themselves stand out or disappear, as desired.

Sometimes a woman will carry a novelty bag which functions like a theatrical prop. It's a conversation piece, chosen to turn heads or act as an ice-breaker. "I know," says one unmarried woman who always takes witty or whimsical bags to parties, "that even if I don't get noticed, my handbag will."

Conversely, a handbag can suppress individuality and help one fade into the crowd. Susan Harrigan, a newspaper reporter in New York City, explains her choice of handbag: "Black, plain, possessed of a paperback-sized pocket. My handbag wasn't anything much until you asked. Now I see it as perfectly expressive of someone who lives in grimy New York, needs to blend in everywhere (as a reporter), and gets stuck on the subway a lot. Oh, and it's always the same (Travelsmith's Hands-Off handbag, in microfiber). Life has too many other complications!"

Many women see psychic parallels with their handbag choices. This is particularly so for women who use essentially only one bag: it must work with her basic identity and lifestyle because she doesn't want the bother of changing it. A college student, Leize Gaillard, primarily relies on a nylon Patagonia bag which she slings over her shoulder. Her keys dangle outside it on a carabiner. In a pinch, she uses the bag as a pillow.

"Some bags are compartmentalized for things like pencils, cell phone, and credit card," she says. "But my personality is not compartmentalized like that. I have one big space I can throw everything into."

Handbags are so tied to identity that using someone else's can make a woman feel like an imposter. Victoria Reggio is a writer in New York whose purse was stolen in a mugging. Until she could buy another, her friend Delores loaned her a brown leather satchel.

Says Victoria: "It was a great bag but it was empty of 'me'; my wallet filled with pictures, good-luck wind-up penguin, prayer beads, and script from the play for which I was planning to audition. I was walking around with Delores hanging from my shoulders. Every time I dug inside, I felt like a fraud. Suddenly, I was supposed to smell like tobacco and patchouli oil?"

So identified are handbags with individuals that sometimes they remain inseparable—for all eternity. The first time I heard about a grandmother being buried with her handbag, I thought I was hearing something unique. But in the course of my research, I heard a surprising number of testimonials about sending a beloved Nana off to heaven with her trusty, omnipresent handbag.

Deborah Moissinac, who lives in New York City, tells this story: "My grandmother, Mary Polinski, died two years ago in her nineties. She always carried a black patent leather bag with a five-inch strap and a metal closure. It never left her side. As a child, I always wondered what was in that bag. Although she probably carried the same five things every woman carries, it was always a mystery.

"Even when she was senile, she had to know where it was. 'Where's my purse?' she would say.

"When she died, we buried her in her pale blue dress holding her purse. She was laid out with the bag at waist point, resting gently on her stomach, with both hands around the handle.

"It was the most precious scene—perfect, perfect."

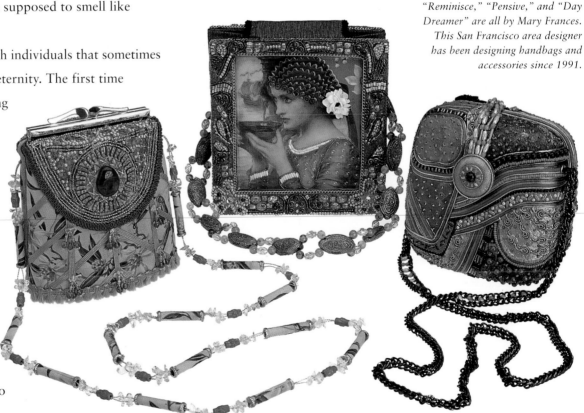

*"Reminisce," "Pensive," and "Day Dreamer" are all by Mary Frances. This San Francisco area designer has been designing handbags and accessories since 1991.*

# IN CHOOSING A PURSE,
## I LOOK AT FUNCTION AND COLOR.
### I ALSO LIKE IT IF THE HANDBAG HAS AN OUTSIDE POCKET.

*But mainly it's whether the purse grabs you.*

## IT CALLS YOUR NAME,
## AND YOU JUST HAVE TO HAVE IT!

—Nancy Small
Licensed tour guide
Charleston, South Carolina

*This decoupaged train case from the 1940s is now a roomy everyday purse for its current owner, who found it in a flea market a few years ago. The train case has a sewing motif featuring dress patterns, vintage models, and labels for thread, needles, and other sewing notions.*

# Lose your handbag and you lose your mind.

—Athene Jordan
Fiber artist

Artist Susan Romaine designed this witty handbag entitled "This Bag is Not a Toy." Its graphic, minatory message is enhanced by its placement on bold, cautionary yellow. This one-of-a kind bag was created to be sold at auction to benefit Charleston, South Carolina's Center for Women.

# IN MY HANDBAG

| TWENTY YEARS AGO | TODAY |
| --- | --- |
| Sunglasses | Reading glasses |
| Midol | Calcium pills |
| Library card | Business card |
| Lip gloss | Liner and lipstick |
| Tiny mirror | Super-magnifying glass |
| Card for dance classes | Gym membership card |
| Charlie spray cologne | Pepper spray |
| Good-luck charm | Mini flashlight |
| Trident | Freedent |
| Breath spray | Altoids |
| Phone book | Palm Pilot |

—Victoria Reggio
American writer

*Appliqués with lively geometric designs kick up the energy of this bold, contemporary handbag in purple and green suede from Christian Livingston.*

Y ou can define a young girl, a woman, or a lady by the handbag she's carrying.

A girl will grab a bag and pack everything into it. It becomes a zip code of its own.

A woman will also carry a bag. She doesn't care what size it is. She'll wear her daytime shoulder bag with an evening dress.

Then there's the lady. She changes her bag with her outfit. It has a handle which she holds in her hand. She understands the total silhouette she creates, and the role her handbag plays in that. She doesn't wear a lumpy bookbag, or carry a bulky piece of luggage.

—Sonya Livingston
Director, Saks Fifth Avenue Club
Charleston, South Carolina

## BOONE COUNTY

3150043

XXX

# Privacy & Secrecy

XXXXXXXXXXXXXXXXXXXXXXXXXXXXXXXXXXXXXXXXXXXXXXXXXXXXXXXXX

*Purses,* like certain areas of the body, are private parts. There's an unwritten rule that you don't go barging into someone's purse uninvited any more than you would trespass that person's physical boundaries. Indeed, so linked are purses to female sexual anatomy that nomenclature for both can be virtually interchangeable: in Shakespeare's time, the English used the term "purse" for vulva; and in the twentieth century the term "old bag" came widely to mean a woman past her sexual prime.

The intimacy between a woman and her handbag arises from their monogamous, often long-term relationship. A woman may have many handbags, but each of them has only one woman: her. Their relationship has all the hallmarks of a good marriage: trust, familiarity, dependability, a shared history, and lots of secret stuff known only to them. The quality of exclusivity is assumed. Just as there should be no sharing of Husband or Significant Other, the handbag is hers and hers alone.

Read the message her body language sends by the way she holds it. She may clutch it like a football, cradle it like an infant, or sling it—guerilla fighter–style, à la Che Guevara—at a diagonal across her body.

What's inside is top secret. The handbag's basic construction is all about concealment. Usually the bag is made of opaque material, impervious to penetrating eyes. It's often closed with a zipper, drawstring, snaps, or metal hardware. Sometimes it even has its own tiny padlock and key.

*Artist Laura Szweda, who lives on an Atlantic coastal barrier island, made this fanciful "Crab Trap" purse with its marine motif from recycled materials, hardware cloth, and bead chain.*

The contents may be sacred or profane, mundane or sublime, ephemeral or permanent.

"Think," muses Harriett Daughtridge of Charleston, South Carolina, "about the possibilities of what you could conceal inside your pocket-book, from a tissue because you are brokenhearted, to the key to your lover's hotel room, to the secret birthday present you are hiding from your child, to incriminating evidence. . . ."

Sometimes efforts at conceal-ment go awry, leaving the handbag owner exposed. One teacher speaks of the time when, laughing uproarious-ly, she inadvertently knocked her handbag over and caused tampons to cascade across the classroom floor, to the hilarity of her students. Another recalls, "I was teaching at an elite school in England when I saw the fascinated, thrilled gaze of my students all converged on one spot at my feet. My hand-bag had fallen from a chair and had spilled condoms all over the floor. It was a great little punch for safe sex, I guess."

The handbag functions as a roving version of a vanity table or bathroom where all sorts of personal rituals can be performed. With deft positioning of head and hands, a woman can "duck into" her handbag, much as she would duck into a powder room if one were available, or if she wanted to. These days, many acts of hygiene or vanity are done publicly, whereas not so long ago they were done behind closed doors.

She's got a mirror for makeup repairs, or for inconspicuous espionage if she wants to check out who just entered a room or party. She can spritz on cologne or hairspray; medicate a sore throat; combat halitosis; or remove her contact lenses. She can file a nail; swallow an estrogen pill; even "wash" her hands with a moist towelette.

*This small pink Buffalo Bag is Carlos Falchi's signature satchel. It won the fashion industry's Coty Award in 1983.*

She depends on her bag to keep her secrets. If she has maxxed out on her credit cards or received a ticket for speeding, only her circumspect handbag need know for sure.

Leslie Pelzer, M.D., emergency room physician, writes of her handbag as her confidante, the *ultimate* Keeper-of-Secrets.

### Purse Verse: Keep It To Yourself, Sister (Or Else)

Some call it a purse:
Some call it a clutch.
Things could be worse
But not by that much.

For my bag is quite lacking
Checks, bank cards, and cash.
Instead it is packing
Wadded tissues, pens, and trash.

But cloaked in opaque leather
She's got a trustworthy look.
I don't worry 'bout whether
She's a blabbermouth pocketbook.

So with a confident demeanor
I toss her over my shoulder.
One word out of her
And it's the trashcan, I scold her.

The antithesis of secrecy is revelation. This is another of the handbag's themes. Sometimes the revelation is quite straightforward, in which the pleasure or surprise derives from the simple unexpectedness of putting ordinary objects on display.

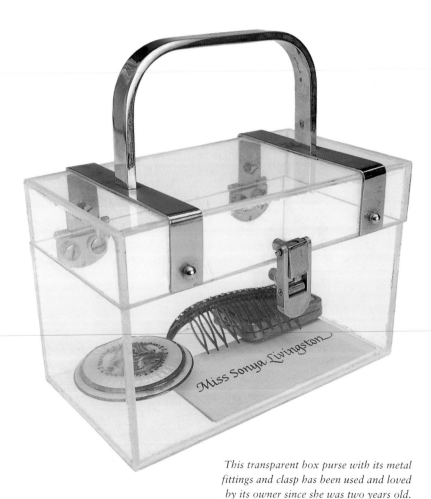

*It is hard to believe that many years ago the present owner's great-grand-mother purchased this gorgeous glass-beaded antique purse for only one dollar. Note the ornate gold frame, double chain handles, and five balls of glass beads dangling from the geometrically-cut bottom.*

Jane McFadden notes that while she is drawn to a workmanlike handbag for daytime, "night choices and considerations are different. The purse can take on a different personality, as there is no need to carry the more serious articles of the day. "Here is my opportunity to enhance an outfit or carry a purse as an object of art or delight. My favorite night purse is a translucent, oval box with a silver clasp and rope handle. It is revealing—generally a small hairbrush, several bobby pins, and a five-dollar bill. Most people are more interested in this revelation than the purse itself."

But sometimes the "revelation" is partial and obscure. The intention is to arouse mystery. The plot thickens. Writes syndicated cartoonist Marian K. Henley, "I have a sack purse made out of sheer purple nylon. Its see-through quality transforms the contents of my purse from the mundanely obvious to the tantalizingly ambiguous—is that a lipstick? Or a tampon? A Kleenex, or a crushed pair of undies? Carrying this purse in public gives me a naughtier thrill than wearing a negligee."

*This transparent box purse with its metal fittings and clasp has been used and loved by its owner since she was two years old.*

*The traditional "Doctor's Bag"
is made of hand-dyed Italian
leather by Oroton.*

A WELL-DESIGNED PURSE, LIKE A GOOD LOUIS XV DESK, SHOULD HAVE A MULTITUDE OF SECRET COMPARTMENTS.

*The interior of a bag is a very private space.*

ONE OF THE MORE UNATTRACTIVE GESTURES A MAN CAN MAKE IS THRUSTING HIS HAND INTO A WOMAN'S PURSE.

—Amy Fine Collins
Special correspondent, *Vanity Fair*

# My handbag is like my lingerie.
## *It's meant only for me.*

—Ann Apple
Photographer and model

*This vintage handbag by Magid has an overlay of bright emerald green chiffon. The original mirror is still inside along with an attached coin purse in green satin. The unusual crown-shaped clasp is still regal and special. Magid has been making handbags since 1916.*

# Purses, I think, are wombs.

*The shape, the darkness, the secrecy,* and all that's hidden away . . .

—Anonymous

*These two beauties by Grace Ann Agostino are newly made but feature her signature reinvented components. The bag on top is of mustard-colored python attached to a French Bakelite frame from the 1920s. The bag in the foreground has a frame made of plastic, from the 1960s. Its luxurious body is made of Italian leather with an unusual marbleized pattern.*

# Power &
# Status

# POWER

Today's alpha woman wields essentially two types of power—secular and seductive—and they are as different as day and night.

By day, she exercises her relatively newly gained power in what used to be strictly a man's world: the workplace. By night, she is no less powerful, but she may—in the intriguing atmosphere of a party or nightclub—revert to that brand of power that has always been hers: her feminine wiles.

Whether she's a politician, scientist, banker, or judge, a serious handbag helps her in two ways. It both ramps up her aura of authority and enhances her performance. From her bag she whips out a Power Point presentation, a laptop, and a Palm Pilot. Wired and in charge, she's got the whole world in her hand.

She would never show up in a pink miniskirt with matching marabou feather handbag to take a deposition or pitch a hedge fund. On the other hand, that same outfit might be just the thing for a different kind of power play at night.

Like a power suit or power car, a power handbag must convey authority, quality, credibility, and trustworthiness. It should be constructed of good quality materials in a standard shape, size, and color. It is a mute ambassador, visually telegraphing a message about its owner. If she wants to lead effectively—or to rise in the hierarchy of the workplace—she knows she must have the right accouterments in her armory.

Two of the most powerful women in the world—Queen Elizabeth II and former Prime Minister Margaret Thatcher, both of England—are strongly identified with their iconic, no-nonsense handbags. The Queen always carries a plain, practical, conservative handbag made by Launer, an English firm. As prime minister, Mrs. Thatcher was legendary for carrying documents and speeches in her black Ferragamo bag, which she liked to place strategically in the middle of a table during Cabinet meetings. The bag recently fetched $150,000 in an Internet auction whose proceeds went to the Breast Cancer Care charity. Observed Samantha Dawe of handbag.com, which organized the auction, to the Associated Press: "It was her icon. It became a symbol of her authority and power the same way as Churchill with his cigar."

The role a handbag plays in achieving traditional power and success can begin before a woman even lands the job. Savvy and ambitious, she knows it's smart to come to the job interview dressed as the kind of employee her future employer is looking for— organized, dependable, discreet. She does not arrive with a ratty bag out of which overflow the effluvia and detritus of a chaotic personality, or the crazy, flamboyant, or bohemian bag which announces that its owner is a diva or an *artiste*. Says Sonya Livingston, handbag aficionada: "I wore my classic black "Lucille de Paris" handbag to an important job interview. My mother had worn it the day I was bat mitvah'd.

*The lipstick red, Hobo shoulder bag displays the signature "O" of its maker, Oroton, a 60-year-old Australian leather goods company. The material is high shine calf leather.*

All these years it has been polished and preserved and taken care of. Later, the interviewer told me she had noticed my bag. I got that job because of it!"

Often a woman will consciously invest in an expensive, versatile handbag, knowing that it will be a powerful ally as she conducts business at home and around the globe. Casey Murphey spent about $1,200 on a classic handbag, the Lady Dior, made by Christian Dior. Named for the late Princess of Wales who favored it, the handbag is made of quilted leather and sports the maker's trademark gold charms dangling handsomely from one of its handles: D, I, O, and R.

Says Casey, who was working as a merchandising consultant in the fashion industry when she bought the bag five years ago: "The fashion industry is image conscious. Insiders know whether something is real or a knock-off. Knock-off is acceptable in some cases, and even a badge of knowledge in that you know what to buy.

"This bag, however, cannot be knocked off. It requires a major machine for its manufacture, lots of labor, exceptionally heavy hardware, inserts in the handles, and, of course, the quilting.

*Chanel's patent leather chocolate bar quilted clutch is a glamorous purveyor of style and status.*

"I needed the bag for traveling and for doing business, especially in the Far East. Carrying the bag helped jump language barriers, and gave me an edge up. I was perceived as a successful businesswoman who was safe to do business with.

"The right handbag is essential in business," says Casey, who uses the same durable, classic Lady Dior in her current job as a realtor. "Mine helps me achieve what I need to achieve. Why not start off on your best foot and not be misassessed?"

## STATUS

A subtext of power is status. The more expensive, luxurious, and unattainable something is, the higher its status, and the keener the desire to possess it. When an object is linked with a royal princess or a movie star, the desire intensifies. This explains how some handbags—like the famous Kelly bag by Hermès—achieve cult status. Hermès named its bag "The Kelly" when Grace Kelly of Philadelphia, a movie star, married Prince Rainier of Monaco in 1955, and overnight became a princess, too. The popularity of the bag really took off when she was later photographed holding it to shield her first pregnancy from the cameras of the paparazzi. Nearly fifty years later, Hermès maintains waiting lists to meet demands for the Kelly bag, one of the most expensive— and desirable—bags in the world.

To carry a status bag—whether it's a Gucci, Fendi, Coach, Chanel, Donna Karan, Prada, to name only a few—is to align oneself with everything the handbag stands for: wealth, good taste, exclusivity, quality. Most women say their choice of a status bag is prompted by an appreciation of superior workmanship and design. Not surprisingly, no one ever says she buys a status bag for the prestige it bestows, though one must imagine that this is often the case.

Often festooned with the designer's initials—the double C's of the Chanel logo; the double F's of the Fendi logo; the entwined LV's of the Louis Vuitton logo—the handbag imparts its maker's status to the wearer. She instantly takes on its chic. "I think," theorizes one woman, "that having such a bag must give the wearer an immediate confidence when she walks into a room or into an unfamiliar situation."

A trio of high-status bags from the distinguished French firm, Louis Vuitton. Note the widely recognized Monogram design: the entwined L's and V's interspersed with crosses and circles. The two bags on the left are new; the one on the right was purchased in Paris in the 1960s.

But for every roomful of women who crave a Moschino, Versace, Longchamps, Lambertson Truex, or other well-made and highly-pedigreed bag, there's one iconoclast whose dream object is unique, handmade, and one-of-a-kind. Norma May is one such person, whose love of wearable art has transformed her into an accessories vendor and connoisseur. Her closet and shop are full of unique bags made of old, born-again Bakelite frames, scraps of antique kimono fabric, recycled ivory, or tortoise shell. Many are hand painted or hand sewn. Norma says, "I couldn't carry any form of production bag, no matter how rare or refined. My love of bags is all about the art form.

"An artist-made or handmade bag is made with love. I read energy when someone has worked on it. The difference is the effort . . . much like the effort it takes to prepare a beautiful meal rather than serve a rotisserie chicken from the grocery store."

What, then, of the fabulous fakes, the designer knock-offs for sale at kiosks on corners in major cities? Women are thoughtful—and careful—about aligning themselves with something that's phony. Misusing a fake status bag can backfire in certain situations. In other situations, though, one can be cheeky and upfront about the chicanery. Says Sandi Mohlmann, a photographer with a wardrobe of serious and playful bags: "I like a knock-off that's obviously a knock-off . . . say, in a color the designer would never use." A reverse snobbery kicks in: the wearer is confident enough to carry an obvious counterfeit.

But when it comes to genuine power and status, only the authentic thing will do. And the scarcer it is—like a Rolls, the Concorde, truffles, or Beluga caviar—the better.

Observes one woman: "Too many copies devalue the desirability of the real thing. Recently my help came to the front door carrying a fake Prada bag. Why have the real thing when your cleaning lady is carrying the knock-off?"

C hatelaine bags of yesteryear were a badge of office announcing that the wearer was <u>head</u> of the household. The daytime bags of contemporary women make a similar statement. She's virtually carrying her walking office, her walking apartment, with her, and like the chatelaine of the castle, she's in charge.

—Carol McLaren
Grandmother

*The khaki linen bag at left with its circular black appliqué has a slightly Asian, Zen-like aura. Its companion to the right in black and neutral toile suggests the other side of the globe: Provençal France. Both are Gianna Costas/San Juan designs.*

# I SHOULD HAVE THE CONFIDENCE NOT TO HAVE TO WEAR LABELS. A BAG SHOULD BE MINE AND NOT BEAR THE NAME OF A DESIGNER.

—Ann Apple
Photographer and model

*This charming, playful, soft green rubber bucket by Salvatore Ferragamo dates from the 1990s. A perfect bag for a summer day, it is reminiscent of a child's pail for playing in the sand.*

AS A YOUNG WORKING GIRL,
I HAD VERY LITTLE TO SPEND ON MY WARDROBE.
THE ONE THING I JUST HAD TO HAVE—
THAT I SCRIMPED AND SAVED FOR—
*was a classic, quilted Chanel handbag.*
MY CLOTHES MIGHT BE ORDINARY
BUT MY BAG HAD TO BE OF THE BEST QUALITY.
IT HAD TO BE THE GENUINE ARTICLE.

—Esther B. Ferguson
Philanthropist

Chanel's classic "2.55" bag, named for its birthday in February 1955, is a masterpiece of refinement. Its famous diamond-shaped quilting and leather-and-chain shoulder strap are recognizable the world over.

Textile artist Paige Hathaway Thorn made this quartet of hand-dyed silk evening bags. The multi-hued bag, which has a pair of translucent beaded handles, has been "obsessively" topstitched, says its designer.

When one sees women carrying status symbol bags—Louis Vuitton, for example—sometimes one doesn't know if they bought them at Saks or from a sidewalk vendor's knock-off pile on the street. Someone gave me a fake Kate Spade bag and it amused me that everyone commented on it—how attractive, how nice, etc. I felt as though I were masquerading as Mrs. Rich Bitch.

—Leila Hadley Luce
Writer and former cartoon editor, *The Saturday Evening Post*

*This heirloom glass-beaded purse with a floral design has a beaded handle and fringe and is attached to a faux-tortoiseshell frame.*

What is considered trash or quality in the South has nothing to do with money. Some of the best families around here haven't had money for generations. No amount of money can make you quality if you don't act like quality. For instance, good southern belles don't place much importance on paying four hundred dollars to buy a pocketbook that's got some Italian designer's initials all over it. In the South, grandmother's monogrammed napkin rings are much more important than Gucci's monogrammed luggage. To think otherwise is just considered tacky. And around here, nothing is more tacky than being tacky.

—Alabama belle discussing the importance of being Southern. Excerpt from *A Southern Belle Primer, Or Why Princess Margaret Will Never Be a Kappa Kappa Gamma* by Marilyn Schwartz
American writer

From *THE IMPORTANCE OF BEING EARNEST*, in which a horrified and haughty Lady Bracknell quizzes Jack Worthing, her daughter Gwendoline's suitor, on his dubious lineage. Jack, a foundling, was discovered as an infant in a handbag many years ago at Victoria Station:

**JACK** (very seriously): Yes, Lady Bracknell. I was in a handbag—a somewhat large, leather handbag, with handles to it—an ordinary handbag, in fact. . . .

**LADY BRACKNELL** (rising): Mr. Worthing, I confess I feel somewhat bewildered by what you have just told me. To be born, or at any rate, bred, in a handbag, whether it had handles or not, seems to me to display a contempt for the ordinary decencies of family life. . . . As for the locality in which the handbag was found, a cloakroom at a railway station might serve to conceal a social indiscretion . . . but it can hardly be regarded as an assured basis for a recognized position in good society. . . . You can hardly imagine that I and Lord Bracknell would dream of allowing our only daughter— a girl brought up with the utmost care—to marry into a cloakroom and form an alliance with a handbag.

—from *The Importance of Being Earnest*
by Oscar Wilde (1854–1900)
Irish author

I'm a handbag snob.
I have a fake Chanel someone gave me
but I don't want it
*because it's not genuine.*
The quality's not there.

—Sonya Livingston
Director, Saks Fifth Avenue Club
Charleston, South Carolina

*On summer holidays in Sicily in the late 1960s, former* Vogue *editor Mary Douglas commissioned expert Sicilian seamstress Marie Louise to make these four lavishly beaded and utterly timeless evening clutches.*

# Glamour & Luxury

*When night falls,* the overtly serious concerns of the day are put away. And so are the sensible handbags.

After dark, the competent businesswoman may morph into a glamorous creature, calling fully on her feminine powers to enchant, seduce, or simply look more beautiful. A major prop in this nocturnal metamorphosis is often her dainty and impractical evening bag. While strides have been made toward achieving gender equality in the workplace, you would never know it from a woman's evening clothes. And although she—tottering on stiletto heels, wearing décolletage, and carrying a tiny bag—may look helpless or powerless, she is anything but!

Such are the paradoxes of the handbag and the woman who carries it. Subtext runs underneath text, meaning underlies meaning. The handbag is a chimera which defies easy categorization. More often than not, it projects several themes or embodies several contradictory meanings at once. The bag may even be said to have multiple personalities.

Thus, the colorful, geometric metal mesh bag by Whiting & Davis, which Nana carried to the speakeasy in the Jazz Age, may connote luxury, status, and nostalgia for the granddaughter who inherited it. It may also confer on her a kind of power in knowing she is descended biologically from a *bon vivante* of good taste and means.

Correspondingly, a CEO's minimalist daytime handbag by Gucci projects status as well as power. Its supple leather, silver grommets, and skilled artisanship certainly betoken luxury. The bag may represent security to her, or be an essential part of her identity.

Every handbag is a kind of lightning rod where all a woman's free floating anxieties, cares, and priorities can go safely to ground!

Like the demure reticules of the past, evening bags are generally smaller, more impractical, and often made of more delicate, rare, or luxurious materials than their daytime counterparts. The best of them qualify as little *objets d'art*.

Lately, evening bags have come out of the closet. Women often display them, either hanging them on the wall like miniature paintings or arranging them like small sculptures in vignettes on coffee tables or étagères. One woman I know collects only vintage beaded clutch-style evening bags. Her collection occupies an entire wall of her living room. Each bag hangs from a tiny, invisible tack; on her way out the door in the evening, she simply selects the bag that best comple-ments her outfit. I recently saw a trio of bags artfully grouped on a table in the home of a professional singer:

*This floral mesh bag, made by Whiting & Davis, resembles a water-color. Founded in 1876 in Massachusetts, Whiting & Davis is one of America's oldest and most venerable handbag manufacturing firms. This circa-1920s heirloom bag has a green enameled frame and an especially feminine scalloped hem. Its lining is bright peach.*

*Designer Cookie Washington created these unique "KISS" bags in the late 1990s. Each is pyramidal in shape, made of luxurious fabric, closed with a zipper, and topped with a fancy tassel.*

an exquisite confection of a silken chambered nautilus; a jaunty evening number topped with Carmen Miranda fruits; and a structured, highly architectural fabric pyramid festooned with a fantastic tassel.

For many women, glamorous evening bags suggest a bygone era of silk stockings, cocktail shakers, and servants. Theresa Cox, a homemaker, inherited two antique bags from her great, great, great grandmother Theresa Fries, born around 1834 or 1835. The fabric bags are attached to sterling silver frames and have been passed down through six generations.

Says the present-day Theresa: "These evening bags represent a time which no longer exists. The women who used them were born to dress up, travel, shop, and give parties. I worked for twenty-five years in a bank. I am retired now, but I still work in the yard, mow the grass, and cook a full meal every day for the family.

"My great-grandmother's journal contains notes on where to buy silk stockings in Rome!"

Harriett Daughtridge says she inherited "glamorous evening bags, jewelry, and my wild spirit" from her great aunt Sadie and two grandmothers, Hallie and Lois. "Great

Aunt Sadie had a home right on the beach in Miami," says Harriett. "These were the days of the Fontainebleau Hotel and horse racing at Hialeah. The tacky people weren't down there yet. The rich people were there. They had a glamorous, glitzy life.

"All these ladies had chauffeurs. Back then, you could take a bath for thirty minutes! Women were afforded the luxury of being pampered ladies. They didn't work, and the help did everything. Around 5:30 or 6:00, the husband came home and she met him at the door, dressed and looking pretty. The kids were bathed and she had his drink and cigarette ready, and it worked!"

Heirloom evening bags do not summon images of glamour for everyone, however. For Cada McCoy, a booklover and equestrienne from Summerville, South Carolina, her antique bags of golden mesh and glass beads suggest lives of stultifying boredom and inertia.

"I had very idle ancestors," she says. "They lived in Delaware. Their lives must have been unbearable. They were served all their meals. They stayed home, napped, and received visitors in the afternoons. The ladies did handwork, and it is possible that my great grandmother did some of the handwork on my antique bags. Their idleness is why I became such a doer!"

Whether evening bags are vintage or new, two other qualities add to their glamorous, luxurious mystique: they are dinky in size, and often made of sumptuous materials.

Luxury is the antithesis of necessity. No one would argue with the fact that you *need* a fairly indestructible handbag to haul around the necessities of your existence, but would anyone agree that you *need* an evening bag in the size and shape of a mouse made of rhinestones and Austrian crystals?

Most evenings bags are so small that they are of limited—or even *zero*—utility. Usually, there's space only for the proverbial lipstick, house key, and credit card. In fact, some women just don't bother. "I like girly things," says one college student, "but they are so little you can't fit anything in there. I just don't see the point!"

In lieu of an evening bag, some women stash indispensables in the pocket of man's tuxedo or suit jacket. Into the husband or date's pocket go the bare essentials such as a comb or pot of lip gloss.

But most women love them because of—not in spite of—their inutility. They are trifles, toys, bibelots, amusements, props, or conversational icebreakers, their very desirability stemming from the fact that they are not so much useful as they are beautiful. What, after all, is more luxurious than something you don't need, which serves no practical purpose, and which basically doesn't do anything except lie around and look pretty?

Whether it's a genuine Judith Leiber minaudière or a vintage brocade clutch from the flea market, the materials and embellishments of a good evening handbag—silks, taffetas, organzas, velvets, tulles, rhinestones, crystals, seed pearls, precious and semiprecious stones, enamels, sterling silver, fourteen-karat gold—offer strong sensory and aesthetic appeal.

Finally, small, glamorous evening bags are usually held in the hand like the reticules of old. Unlike bigger, bulkier day-bags, sportsacs, rucksacks, or totes, they do nothing to destroy the elegant line of the wearer's contours.

Says Amy Fine Collins of *Vanity Fair:* "The best bags are crisp and neat in silhouette; they should never destroy the line of the clothes. That is why short-handled purses, borne on the arm or wrist, are more elegant than those equipped with shoulder straps. Worse than saggy shapeless bags are backpacks, which turn a woman, at best, into a beast of burden, and, at worst, a hunchback. It's better to be bagless than to resemble a coalminer's mule."

*This pair of heirloom purses on ornate sterling silver frames once belonged to Theresa Fries, who was born in the nineteenth century. The frame at left features an elaborate design based on the King Neptune myth. Note the musical mermaids. The back of this frame is engraved "T. Fries— Rock Island, Ill." The frame at right has a Cupid theme on both its front and back.*

*This glass-beaded, antique pansy purse with its beaded wrist strap and extraordinarily vivid color has lost none of its charm and winsomeness over the years. It has been cherished by the current owner's family for several generations. She speculates it may even have been made by an ancestor during the days that women did fancywork at home.*

I know my Columbo handbag is the best in the world. I know for a fact.

I own lots of Hermès bags, because I decorated two apartments for Hermès. They are the most luxurious. The insides are like babies' bottoms.

I own several from Mr. Renaud; they have lipstick holders sewn in every handbag, but nothing compares to my Columbo bags. I love them so much that I bought three: black with camel lizard flap, brown with brown lizard flap, and navy with navy lizard flap. They look small, but they hold a standard yellow pad. They are not deep so you can always put your hands on your wallet in a hurry. The zipper compartment is large enough to hold a plane ticket. They are so chic and timeless.

I also love the flat cord evening bags from Paris that come in fifteen colors and pack weightlessly. And all the hand needlepointed bags that Dey used to make. But on the weekend I only carry a straw bag from Seventh Avenue. It is made in Japan and anyone who sees it walks over to Fifty-eighth and buys one from the man who sells only one product—my second favorite bag.

—Stephanie Stokes
Interior designer

# . . . WE WOULD WEAR
## GOLD CHAINS AND DIAMOND TIARAS,
## AND IN OUR PLANS WE HAD THE
# PURSE OF FORTUNATUS
## AND THE LUCK OF ALADDIN'S LAMP.

—Margaret E. Sangster (1838–1912)
American author and editor of *Harper's Bazaar*

*This Victorian glass-beaded pouch bag
has a fancy filigreed frame and beaded
wrist strap. Of the many handbags in her
vast collection, this one is the owner's
most prized possession.*

# The gorgeous handbags

I inherited hark back to a time when

## *ladies were ladies*

and glamour was the game.

—Harriett Daughtridge
Mother, avid traveler, civic volunteer

The bag on the left is made of metal beads with a mother-of-pearl button clasp, generous fringe, and a design that is both Moorish and Art Deco in feeling. On the right is a glass beaded evening purse with an intricate floral design, mounted on a silver frame and finished with looped fringe in alternating colors. The small, flat, black purse with its fantastic birds and foliage was made in Austria, possibly in a convent, of finest petit point. All three bags are family heirlooms from around the 1920s.

*Chrome handles, caviar beading,
and dyed hackle feathers ornament
this pair of MooRoo evening bags.
"Rio Flamingo" is at left and
"Rio Ocean" is at right.*

RECENTLY, FOUR FRIENDS WENT TO PARIS
**AND BROUGHT ME BACK A GIFT.**
EVEN THE SHOPPING BAG IT WAS PRESENTED IN—HEAVY,
GLOSSY, WHITE PAPER EMBOSSED IN GOLD—WAS IMPRESSIVE.
TUCKED INSIDE WAS A TINY,
BEAUTIFULLY CRAFTED, AND WILDLY IMPROBABLE
**EVENING BAG,**
MADE OF LOOK-AT-ME ORANGE SILK SHIMMERY
ENOUGH TO QUALIFY AS DAY-GLO,
**TOO SMALL TO CONTAIN**
MUCH MORE THAN A PACK OF BREATH MINTS,
AND UTTERLY IMPRACTICAL.

*I loved it!*

—B.G.S.
American writer

The inside of my grandmother's pocketbook smelled like Arpege mixed with Pepomint LifeSavers (she always had a roll, supplied from a box of them in her top dresser drawer). There was a lace-edged handkerchief, too. I don't remember a wallet, although there must have been one.

In her era, my grandmother had little use for cash and credit cards. Groceries were added to her account and dress shops simply "sent the bill." Everybody knew her. My own purse, today, is bulging with ATM slips, credit cards, debit cards, "valued customer" cards. It's a far cry from the elegant, composed interior of my grandmother's purse—and it says a lot about how the world has changed.

—Constance Costas
American writer

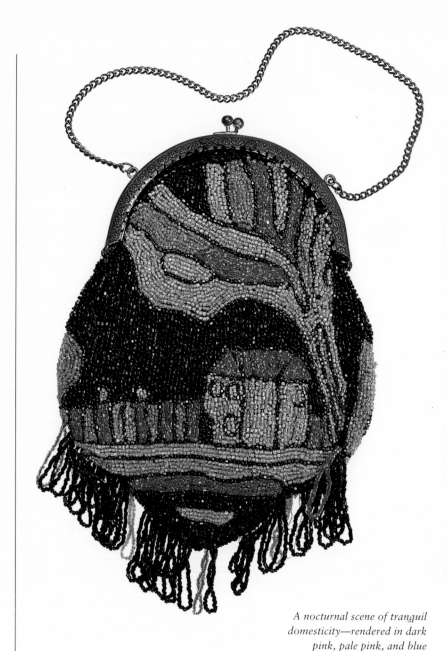

*A nocturnal scene of tranquil domesticity—rendered in dark pink, pale pink, and blue glass beads—is portrayed on this old purse.*

# YOU CAN'T MAKE A *silk purse* OUT OF A SOW'S EAR.

—Old proverb

*Hundreds of brilliant round rhinestones ramp up the glamour of this evening bag on a black enamel frame which the owner inherited from her grandmother. "When I wear my diamonds, this is the bag I carry," she says.*

# Memory & Nostalgia

*Time and space* travel have nothing on a handbag's power to whisk a woman back to another time and place. Unclasping the bag is like taking the cap off a whistling kettle: genies of memory escape.

Whether antique, vintage, heirloom, or merely "last year's," handbags have the power to conjure a specific person, time gone by, or past event. The metaphors abound: they are time capsules, reliquaries, hope chests, or archives that hold memories within their charmeuse seams or gilt frames.

*Marked "Brevité," this solid gold antique purse was made in France and has a diminutive satellite coin purse. Both "live" inside a bank vault, from which they are liberated for very special occasions by their owner. The purse was one of three acquired by the family at an auction (probably Sotheby's) in New York City around 1930.*

Most strikingly, handbags can powerfully summon the essence of the person who once carried it. The first time I witnessed this phenomenon I was visiting a woman who held her deceased mother's clutch-style Sunday purse in her lap. It still contained her mother's tissues, bus schedule, religious medal, and a spool of thread whose color the mother had intended to match. Just as an elderly mother might have been, the purse itself was a bit frumpy and old-fashioned. It had a classical female shape, snap closure, and sturdy fabric body. All the contents were intact, frozen in time just as the mother had left them thirty years ago. When the daughter opened the handbag and displayed each of these talismans to me, I, too, became aware of the absent mother. Her essence had been released just as the scent of perfume pours from a flacon, suddenly decanted.

For some women, objects trigger intense associations—the sudden sight of a grandmother's nitroglycerine pills, or the scent of her Chanel Number 5 still imbedded in the weave of her Belgian lace handkerchief. For other women, her attitude toward her handbag is a revealing prism through which she can view her relationship with her own mother.

Rosemary Daniell is a poet and novelist who lives in Savannah, Georgia. Her award-winning memoir, *Fatal Flowers*, is a searching inquiry into the lives of her own mother and herself. Observes Rosemary:

"I sometimes envy friends who carry tiny purses that look like jewelry or small works of art, and the ones who carry no purse at all, instead going out into the night with a lipstick and keys in one pocket, a money clip in another. But I know I am not, and never will be, one of those.

"My mother, Melissa, was a beautiful Southern woman who was also a brilliant writer who thought she didn't have the right to be. She was also a woman who refused to go anywhere without her purse—always one of the large rectangular kind with a strap. Once, Mother even carried her purse as we climbed Onion Mountain behind the North Carolina farmhouse where she had moved from Atlanta to live with her second husband.

"What did she carry in that bag she carried so obsessively? Crumpled Kleenex, bobby pins, her checkbook, a brush for her thick

*Sweet-faced hounds and foxes peer out from their backdrop of berries and leaves in this appealing clutch. The needlepoint was done by the owner's grandmother in 1968, then sent to New York where it was professionally attached to a frame and converted to a handbag.*

naturally curly hair? I have no idea. But by then, she had already had several of the 'nervous breakdowns' that would soon lead to her suicide, and I considered her obsessive attachment to her purse a part of her general dis-ease. Indeed, at that time, as a young woman and the twice-married mother of three, I was determined to lead a life as different as hers as possible.

"But now, almost three decades later, I find myself carrying a purse just as large and just as compulsively as she did. And though mine contains the things I consider essential to, and even decorative of, my life goals—a pink mesh bag containing the many-colored (cerise, green, purple) pens with which I like to sign books and critique manuscripts, an antique embroidered case for makeup, some loose costume jewelry, a little case for a folding toothbrush and paste, not just one notebook, but several, address book, checkbooks, receipts, and now, even a Smart Input—a translucent turquoise keyboard with memory, almost light as a compact, from which I can download 100 pages of a single-spaced text into my I-Book (my first thought when I saw it and fell in love with it at a writer's conference was: it will fit in my purse! *And* it's pretty!).

"So how different am I from Mother? The world might say, a great deal. But I know in my heart I am no freer of the compulsion to carry large parts of my life along with me than Mother was. And my accepting that is a part of my accepting the beautiful parts of what she gave me, as well as the rest."

*This slightly damaged but still appealing antique bag was purchased for a few dollars in a flea market in Austin, Texas. Its tiny beads are hand-sewn onto a black fabric body in a swirling, abstract pattern. The bag has a double-hinged, ornate metal frame and a simple chain handle.*

So strongly associated are handbags with people or memories that many a woman has difficulty parting with them, even if the bags are so dumpy or damaged that she knows she'll never use them again. She *cannot* bring herself to call the Salvation Army or Goodwill. Somehow, those bags *are* Mother, and to throw them out is unthinkable!

For some women, pocketbooks summon memories of their younger selves. A New Jersey woman, Natalie Margolis, whose grandfather was a handbag manufacturer in Manhattan from the late 1940s to early 1950s, remembers that her grandfather made child-sized versions of stylish bags to match her every outfit. "My guess is that he made me the pocketbooks as soon as I was old enough to walk. I was an only child and my mother always dressed me in the latest child fashion of the time. We were not wealthy, but I never lacked for anything—I had

hats, coats, and leggings outfits for the winter, with handbags to match."

Her favorites had felt appliqués of dogs and lollipops. Natalie remembers her grandfather as a very special man. "He had nineteen grandchildren and each one felt as if he or she was the favorite. These pocketbooks were only for me; the others had their own special things."

Like conjurors, old handbags may evoke nostalgia. They come equipped with powerful Proustian stimuli: olfactory, visual, tactile. One whiff of April Violets or Wint-o-green LifeSavers or even the mustiness of the attic or cedar chest can send a woman on a swift magic carpet ride back in time.

Lee Hilton is a New Jersey writer who inherited a collection of evening bags from her grandmother, including "a black bag brocaded with fruits, a sparkling gold clutch with a rhinestone clip, a pearly white beaded bag, a silver mesh sack (vintage 1920s) on a thin silver chain, and an intricately woven, off-white purse with a bone ring attached to the zipper."

Recently, when cleaning out a drawer, Lee came across the collection. The off-white purse was on top of the stack. "Picking it up, I hooked my finger through the bone ring, and unzippered the center pouch. Inside was a small, gold compact, the kind ladies used to fill with loose powder. I popped it open, and the scent of powder there took me straight back to her huge bedroom in the big stone house she inhabited alone for almost fifty years. She'd sit on the needlepointed bench in front of her dressing table and 'put on her face' in a ritual that was pretty much the same as long as I knew her. 'A lady never goes out without her face,' she'd say in that soft Southern voice that never quite lost its hints of small-town Louisiana. And then she'd add, 'Besides, I wouldn't want to scare anyone, now, would I?'"

Oftentimes, a beloved handbag can summon a special occasion: bat mitzvah or sweet sixteen, debutante party, wedding, a divorce, a raise or bonus, anniversary, an exotic trip, a summer in Italy. If it is already a family heirloom, the owner may choose to add more history of her own, by carrying it, for instance, to a grandchild's baptism.

Or she may set about creating an heirloom of her own. Says Ann Apple, who remarried six years ago: "For my second wedding, I discovered that the purse I wanted to have with me that day was already in my drawer. It's a little antique drawstring bag that I bought at an antique fair twenty-five years ago. It is cream-colored and hangs on the wrist like a bracelet. Its silk lining is torn. It has become my own heirloom now that the history of my wedding ceremony is incorporated into it. I plan to pass it on to my daughter."

For Sonya Livingston, a silk evening bag made by Tano of Madrid always takes her back to a family trip in 1959 to New York City. That day, her father purchased the bag—which depicts Fragonard's romantic painting *The Girl on a Swing*—as a gift for her mother. On their way to see the film *Gigi* at Radio City Music Hall, Sonya got her hand caught in a door and started crying, so her father bought her the matching wallet, which also pictures *The Girl on a Swing*.

"Whenever I look at them," says Sonya, "I can still hear my father singing 'Gigi.'"

Sometimes handbags function as small, private, ambulatory museums. Stuff collects and accretes at the bottom, forming layer upon archeological layer: ticket stubs from a performance of *Cosi Fan Tutte* at the opera, a Matisse exhibit at the MOMA, a concert starring Kurt Cobain, strange, square-shaped foreign coins, or useless paper money engraved with the visages of dictators or kings.

Television critic and purse connoisseur Mindy Spar says, "My bags serve as travelogues, memory keepers, archives, or diaries. I keep money and ticket stubs. I still have coins from a trip to Estonia and when I open that bag I remember traveling in Russia, I remember the train, the countryside. . . .

"I have stubs from an *NSync concert and Alvin Ailey performance, and I also have my grandmother's bowling league card from the '50s, which I'll never throw out."

Last but not least, handbags can yield not only memories but also actual, wonderful, adored objects that had gone missing, such as the A.W.O.L. ivory comb or telephone number jotted on a napkin that you thought was lost forever in the Bermuda Triangle of your life.

Writes Ellen Levine, the editor-in-chief of *Good Housekeeping* magazine: "My bag is like a personal treasure chest—I never know what I am going to find. Loose change, earrings I thought I lost, Tiffany pens missing for years."

Just last night I was house cleaning and found three of my mother's purses that had been her favorite for the last few years. She has Alzheimer's and lives near us now much to the dislike of her independent spirit. Her purse for years now has been her symbol of purpose, independence, and security. Whenever it has been out of her sight either through her hiding it or losing it, she has panicked.

Last night, as I found them stuck back in my hall closet, I wept. I took them out and sat on the floor in the foyer and pulled out wallets full of scraps of paper with former business contacts that filled her life. Literally fifty or more "reasons to mail in this coupon so she would win the million dollar sweepstake." Car keys that were symbols of power and escape from all of us "interfering in her life." Never without her bright red lipstick, dozens of tubes worn down in the exact same pattern by her daily lip painting ritual. Checks written out to cash stuffed secretly in pockets and

*Tall, stylized, silvery leaves embellish this glass-beaded vintage pocketbook with an intricate filigreed frame. The interior is lined in midnight-blue satin.*

crevices, dozens and dozens of reminders to herself so she might keep appearing in control. The insides of the purses as messy and disheveled as her mind had become. I cried as I remembered those Italian bags when they were new with a bright silk scarf tied jauntily around the strap . . . off to new adventures. I kissed them, and then put them in the trash can, trying to let one more thing go gently into the night.

—Fredda Culbreth
Real estate developer, writer

# MORE THAN A POCKETBOOK

## (THE HANDBAG AS AN EMBLEM OF A RITE OF PASSAGE)

I remember when I bought my first *real* pocketbook, a grown-up pocketbook like our mothers carried. It was 1959, I was in the seventh grade, and my baby-sitting money of $0.50 an hour was hoarded preciously. I needed to save $15.00 for the Etienne Aigner pocketbook I had chosen at the Porgy and Bess dress shop: a lovely straw, Nantucket-like fisherman's basket with mahogany-colored leather straps and brass fittings. Proud is inadequate to describe the way I felt as the new owner of this wonderful grown-up pocketbook. I was the envy of my friends. It was my treasure, and as such, it was well cared for and well loved.

I used that pocketbook through most of high school and then retired it to the closet shelf. That pocketbook had marked a rite of passage for me into the world of adult accessories, and I couldn't bring myself to throw it away. My fisherman's basket pocketbook remained in the closets of my life in college, through many moves in early marriage and into mid-life until one day when my daughter, Katharine, discovered it hiding in the closet. A grown woman about to be married to a fly fishing guide, Katharine wanted the pocketbook for a wall hanging in her home in Jackson Hole, Wyoming. She was thrilled with her find . . . a treasure all over again. The fisherman's basket pocketbook now has a new life, in a place of honor on the wall of Katharine's home for the world to admire again. In her dotage, this beautiful old pocketbook continues to be the envy of Katharine's friends.

—Ginny Good
Educational development director and artisan

# Memory is like a purse—
## if it be overfull that it cannot shut,
# all will drop out of it.

—Thomas Fuller (1608–1661)
British clergyman, author, and wit

*This vintage brown alligator purse, of a style popular in the 1940s and 50s, is surmounted by claws with talons, a handsome metal clasp, and a single braided leather handle. The religious artifacts that once belonged to the present owner's grandmother are still safely stored inside.*

I have a little beaded purse that belonged to my Great Aunt Sara . . . I have kept that purse for years and moved it every time I packed up for a new home. When I open my little 'memento drawer' and see that purse, I get a sense of belonging to a family. When I open the purse, I remember Sunday dinners, playing cards, going to church, and laughter. That little purse is like a gateway in my heart to what childhood should be like. I only wish I could find time to open that purse every day.

—Joyce Nelson
Technical consultant

*Blue, aquamarine, and pale mocha-
colored beads encrust this vintage
clutch by Magid, giving it the look
of an Impressionist painting.*

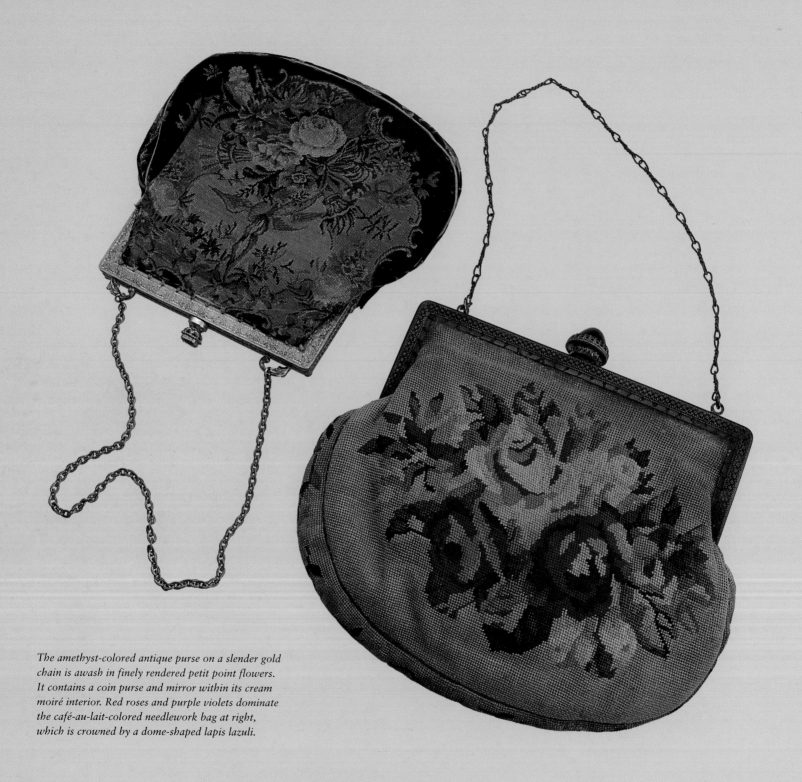

The amethyst-colored antique purse on a slender gold chain is awash in finely rendered petit point flowers. It contains a coin purse and mirror within its cream moiré interior. Red roses and purple violets dominate the café-au-lait-colored needlework bag at right, which is crowned by a dome-shaped lapis lazuli.

*I love my old handbags.* ONE TRANSPARENT ONE I HAVE HAD SINCE AGE TWO. I'M SUCH A HOPELESS ROMANTIC AND SENTIMENTALIST. YOU CAN BUY NEW BAGS BUT THEY COULD NEVER HOLD THE MEMORIES THAT MY OLD ONES DO.

—Sonya Livingston
Director, Saks Fifth Avenue Club
Charleston, South Carolina

# Vulnerability & Security

*A common theme* among women pertaining to handbags is security and vulnerability. Sometimes women describe their handbags as a *literal* means to survival; other times, as a *psychic* means. Regardless of individual interpretation, handbags loom large in a woman's defense systems.

First and foremost is the simple fact of the bag's existence, knowing its location, and being able to put one's hand on it instantly. After all, the bag empowers her to face life and all its surprises, brickbats, and curve balls.

When I was a child of eleven, my family and I took a cruise on an ocean liner to South America. Aboard ship, I met a woman who made an indelible impression on me. As we spoke one day, the woman confided to me that she never went anywhere without her supply of solid gold. She opened her purse and, to my amazement, pulled out a small jar full of gold nuggets. "You never know what's going to happen," she explained. "Gold is a form of international currency that is valued all over the world. I always have it just in case of an emergency."

Several times in my purse explorations I've heard variations on this theme—that something dire may occur, and a woman wants to be able to flee on a moment's notice. It may be just "the date from hell" she wants to be able to escape, or it may be a country or inflamed political situation. Some women always have their passport in their handbag; others, "enough" money, whatever that sum may mean to a particular individual; others, jewelry. (It is astounding how much valuable jewelry is stuffed inside handbags. I had dinner recently at a restaurant with an old friend I'd not seen in years. She has a small business as a jewelry designer, and casually pulled out about $20,000 worth of rings from her handbag to show me. Conversely, I know a woman who keeps her jewelry in a vault at a nearby bank. When she wants to wear a piece to a black-tie gala, she transports it to and from her home not in a purse, but in an ordinary paper bag, on the theory that no thief is going to snatch a brown paper bag!)

At the very least, the loss of a bag and its contents subject the owner to the unpleasant prospect of dealing with beaurocracy until she replaces everything. At the very worst, such a loss may actually strand a woman, at least for a while. No wonder a woman may feel anything from a mild disturbance to an all-out panic if she can't locate her handbag.

Says one woman: "The thought of losing my purse gives me terrible anxiety. I've had panics about where my purse is, so now I make a point of taking it to bed with me every night."

*Sarah Blessing recently made this petite evening bag of olive silk. It has two delicate, beaded handles and tiny bead detail at both top and bottom.*

*This tribal satchel sends a bold message about feminine strength. It is embellished by fierce female visages, wild fringe, shiny mirrors, colored plastic beads, and cowrie shells, long a symbol of female power. It was made by artist Kelly Chambers.*

On the flip side, the presence of the handbag can be extraordinarily reassuring, as another woman's story dramatically illustrates. This woman had just endured the trauma of her husband's terminating their twenty-year marriage. Shortly after, the historic old mill she'd been painstakingly restoring for almost as many years, burned, uninsured, to the ground. In the fire she lost both the mill and all her cherished objects: gorgeous old Venetian mirrors, antique furniture, and vintage Fortuny fabrics. "My first thought," she recounts of this second devastation, was, *'Thank God, I still have my dress and my purse.'"* In the midst of catastrophe and loss, a woman's instinct is for self-preservation. She dead reckons what she absolutely must have, bottom line, to survive.

At its most literal level, the handbag can be deployed as an actual weapon against muggers (perish the thought!) or unwanted suitors. I know a woman who lived for a time in Rome and routinely fended off advances by unknown Romeos on the street with her clutch purse. Boxy alligator

purses, chain metal bags, slim envelope-style bags all have been used by women as light artillery in life's skirmishes.

Women have evolved in their street smarts, and in the evolving have developed their strategies for self-protection. In huge metropolises like New York City, they often wear their bags slung at a military diagonal across their bodies, the better to thwart purse snatchers. Some women want their hands free, should the need arise; others feel more powerful with a handbag in hand.

Writes Tyler Scott: "I don't know why—and I'm sure a psychiatrist would have a heyday with this one—but I actually prefer carrying a handbag because I love the image of me getting bothered by someone and THWAP! I bean them over the head with my lovely Ferragamo bag. A shoulder bag just isn't the same. It bounces under your arm like a piece of overripe fruit, but a handbag—firm, shiny leather with a few well-placed buckles—can be a weapon. Look out! Holly Golightly has a mean hook!"

Just as a handbag can be used as a weapon of attack by a woman, it can be used as a shield *against* attack. Again, heaven forbid having to do so, but many a handbag has been hoisted by a woman warrior to deflect an assailant. Handbags can be used as battle shields, in either physical or psychological battles. One woman tells of having to face a much-dreaded battle in a courtroom. She borrowed from a friend a "much-repaired Indian bag spangled with patchwork, mirrors, and cowrie shells." Cladding herself almost as a shaman, she not only "borrowed" power from her supportive friend but also drew animistically on the primitive power of mirrors and shells to shield herself in court.

Although most women never have to use their handbag in a literal battle, all regard the bag as, on some level, a portable survival kit. Anne Benjaminson is a student at Berkeley in California who sees her bag as "a roving support system—it contains whatever weapons one needs to face life: chapstick, cell phone, sunglasses, post-its with address of where I'm going, loose change. . . . And why leave out the 'how did that get in there' aspect: old pictures, something you were carrying for your boyfriend. I have about three bags I use on weekends. On Friday, they are neatly stacked in a closet. By Sunday, they are strewn, half-empty, about the room."

A mother's handbag is perhaps more indispensable than anyone's. Very often it contains the survival tools necessary not only for herself but also for members of her tribe, her family. Women are relational beings and are hardwired, far more than men, for the survival and sustenance of the human race, especially of the young. Athene Jordan of Summerville, South Carolina, is one such mother. She custom-makes enormous fabric satchels which contain everything except the proverbial kitchen sink. Says Athene of her deep, cavernous bag: "I can pack enough clothes in here for three people for two days. I can even fit a quilt inside."

Another mother tells of an emergency situation in which her handbag served as a calming presence. Emily Abedon is a freelance writer in Charleston, South Carolina, and the mother of three young girls. One day, quite suddenly, her six-month-old infant began throwing up and choking. "It was terrifying," writes Emily, "and my heart was racing as I got her into the car seat and drove toward her pediatrician.

I might have run out without my pants on for as discombobulated as I felt. But, as always, I grabbed my trusty handbag. I glanced over at it lying next to me in the passenger seat and I imagined it calling out 'shotgun!' like we always did as kids. And I felt a tiny surge of relief and calm knowing that it was there beside me, dependably over-packed and predictable, even when nothing else is."

Adds Emily: "The other thing I thought was pretty cool about my handbag was that it contained all the other parts of me that had nothing to do with the wild-eyed woman I'd transformed into. There (though tucked away for the moment) was my makeup bag (evidence of a woman who has a minute to think about her appearance), my Filofax (filled with indisputable proof that I have a career—sometimes!), a notebook and pen (the spontaneously creative gal I dream of being has to be equipped), and even perfume (which speaks for itself)."

*Sleek and uncluttered, this fabric bag by Salvatore Ferragamo sports double handles, classic metal hardware, and a slender bucket shape. It was purchased by its owner in New York City in 2000.*

For centuries and centuries there has been the archetype of Mother Earth, the nurturer and provider. Whereas men have been more externally-oriented, women have always been more attuned to relationships with others. Women are much more the source of maintaining the emotional life of those around them, and the purse helps them do this. Think of the simple act of having tissues available in the purse for herself and others. In the modern age, men seem to have quit carrying handkerchiefs, but you'll rarely catch a woman without a tissue in her purse.

—Sally W. Smith, M.D.
Psychiatrist

*Emerging new designer Gianna Costas of Gianna Costas/San Juan immediately thought of "the American picnic table" when she first saw this cheerful silk taffeta fabric in blue and red checks. Deep and short-handled, these purses are made to be carried in the hand.*

# CHILDHOOD PURSES

They were tiny purses, and they were filled with money. They were red hard plastic, and the "money" was chocolate coins wrapped in gold foil. I remember having one of these purses with me often in kindergarten class. My aunt gave them to me, and they were a comfort—especially during the first scary days of school. Though there have been many purses since then with real money within, none have provided such a sense of security as those first "handbags."

—Ellen E. Hyatt
Professor of English

# PURSE ANXIETY

You know what I'm talking about. You're sitting in a restaurant, perhaps in mid-sentence, when you suddenly gasp and thrust your hand under the table to make sure your purse is still there. It is, of course. You knew it would be but still you feel a flood of relief. Now you can get on with your lunch, your conversation, your life.

It happens so fast that you don't even know what's going through your mind beyond a brief mental "Oh-oh!" followed by that blessed feeling that all is again right with the world. Balance has been restored. God is in his heaven and your purse is under the table.

—Katie Sullivan
American writer

# TO ME THE MOST REASSURING
## CHARACTERISTIC OF A PURSE IS ITS TANGIBILITY.

# *You feel it, touch it, hold it.*

## YOU DEPEND ON YOUR PURSE,
## AND ITS SHEER PHYSICALITY CONFIRMS IT'S THERE FOR YOU.

—Gervais Hagerty
Student

*The yellow raw silk clutch with
its sea anemones and leaves is a
work of art that was purchased in
an antiques shop for fifteen dollars.
Its embellishment of thick, intricate
gold and silver threads has been
exquisitely rendered by anonymous hands.*

# Fun, Frivolity & Fantasy

**Sometimes** girls just want to have fun. And when serious fun is on the agenda, there is no better co-conspirator than a kicky handbag!

A fun, frivolous bag announces a lighthearted attitude. The wearer may feel frisky and extroverted: she wants to be noticed. She may want to charm or amuse with her novelty bag. Or perhaps she wants to indulge a flight of fancy, or make a statement that she is adventurous, or even wild, free, and *available*. Whatever bit of live theatre is being staged, the right handbag is an invaluable prop.

"Bags," observes Sandi Mohlmann, a photographer and interior designer living in Charleston, South Carolina, "are a means of self expression. For fun, for mystique, for a kick, it's delightful to show up in something out of the ordinary."

Walking into a party, luncheon, or college reunion carrying a handbag in the shape of a dragonfly, television set, or birdcage is guaranteed to set the wearer apart and establish a mood of mirth. Whether the bag is a fanciful work of art with a hefty price tag, like Judith Leiber's iconic minaudières, or whether it's a recycled or improvised piece the wearer cobbled together or bought for pennies at a garage sale, at no time in the past have handbags been more fun, more diverse, and more subject to lively interpretation by both professional designers and creative dressers alike.

Fun and wacky motifs abound in purse design. Novelty purses—in the shapes of champagne buckets, poodles, or cruise liners—have been in vogue almost since the advent of the modern handbag. Creative adaptations are rampant, and often utilize discarded cultural materials such as car license plates or beer cans. There is virtually no limit to what may become a purse: an old, hollowed-out camera, gas mask, doll, stuffed animal, shellacked magazine folded lengthwise and fitted with straps, and more.

"I like interesting bags, unusual bags. The shell of an armadillo, for example, used as a bag—attached with real silver chains, the contents covered with a silk scarf—was a great success one summer. I stopped a Guatemalan on the road and haggled for the bag when I first saw it, and was delighted to be able to buy it for a price satisfactory to the man carrying it and to me."

—Leila Hadley Luce
Writer and former cartoon editor, *The Saturday Evening Post*

Traditional feminine iconography—flowers, birds, houses, nests, fruits, and other symbols of fertility and domesticity—often occurs in fun handbags. On the casual end are straw baskets festooned with silk flowers; small, decoupaged picnic hampers; whimsical straw houses or barns; or retro kiddy lunch kits.

More valuable, and also ultra feminine, are the luxurious handbags of designers

*The little straw house with its steep-pitched roof and short plastic handle was made, and purchased, in Japan over fifty years ago.*

such as MooRoo and Judith Leiber. MooRoo, a newcomer whose real name is Mary Norton, burst on the scene when one of the first handbags she designed was chosen—through a series of lucky flukes—by actress Julia Louis-Dreyfus to be worn to the Fiftieth Annual Emmy Awards. The photo of Julia carrying MooRoo's pink silk orchid confection appeared in *People* magazine, *USA Today*, and the *Los Angeles Times*, and MooRoo's career was launched. This designer makes lavish use of feathers and beads, and titles each of her fantasy bags—Palazzo Peacock, Ice Tray, Julia, Sushi Roll, Breakfast at Tiffanies—much as an artist would a painting.

Costlier still are the legendary evening bags of Hungarian-born handbag designer Judith Leiber, perhaps the greatest of handbag designers living in America today. Although Leiber also makes handbags for daytime, she is best known for her minaudières, hard-cased small evening bags that combine the functions of

*MooRoo's "Breakfast at Tiffanies" (left) displays an extravagance of glossy coque feathers. The purse was inspired by Audrey Hepburn's performance in the film* Breakfast at Tiffany's. *"Sushi Roll," at right, owes its design inspiration to sushi itself. The plain fabric bag has been overlaid with natural bamboo, a Japanese symbol for good luck.*

handbag, compact, and jewelry. Each glittering bag may feature anywhere from 7,000 to 13,000 Swarovski crystals, each painstakingly glued on by hand. And although these gemlike bags exude glamour, they also embody the themes of fun, frivolity, and fantasy all at once, depicting whimsical, bejeweled versions of butterflies, monkeys, cats, fans, snakes, cats, polar bears, doves, rosebuds, elephants, dogs, Fabergé eggs, and a host of motifs aligned with feminine beauty and fertility.

I met a woman whose husband has been giving her at least one or two Leibers a year for years. Like most Leiber collections, hers has a theme. The theme she has chosen is animals, and her collection has grown to over thirty handbags, which she displays in an illuminated, mirrored vitrine in her bedroom. Preferring to enjoy her dazzling miniature zoo on a daily basis, she refuses to put the collection under lock and key, or in a vault at the bank.

"It's my happy thing," she says. "If I have a down day, I turn on the light and look at them and smile. As Martha Stewart would say, my collection of Leibers is 'a good thing,'" she says.

Sometimes flashes of wit are displayed via handbags. The traditional, somewhat boxy "alligator purse" is subject to witty re-interpretation, and has been reincarnated more than once as a soft amphibian with handles, a toothy grin, and a zipper running down its back. The Italian designer Moschino is known for witty bags: one memorable bag is made of white leather with rich brown "chocolate" dripping

*Like this beguiling Humpty Dumpty, each Judith Leiber contains a tiny golden mirror and tasseled comb within. The legendary Leiber began her handbag business in New York in 1963.*

down its side. And some witty artists and seamstresses are attracted to the play of words in "hand" bag: I have seen several soft "hands" fitted with handles and carried as purses.

If purses are a female obsession, so too, sometimes, is food. The obsession doubles when food becomes the purse's motif. Deborah Moissinac of New York City is a professional designer who also makes one-of-a-kind purses for special occasions just for herself. For her birthday, she made a version of a birthday cake purse. Some of Moissinac's other fun food bags include a strawberry cheesecake and two sunny-side-up fried eggs atop a lettuce leaf and slice of bread.

Sometimes handbag humor takes a screwball turn. Goofy, eccentric materials or crazy forms ratchet up the insanity: there are bags made from used car parts or intricately-woven, discarded cigarette packages; bags embellished with old-fashioned bottle caps or teeth; bags shaped like angels' wings or ice cream cones.

If the handbag is fun, the dialogue or reaction it generates can be even more so. Nancy Smythe, a poet and grandmother, likes to carry a nontraditional bag to church. The bag is hand-painted silk, and depicts a cat and a mouse. "Some people in church look at me askance," says Nancy. "I know they are thinking: is she crazy? Their reaction—that's the part I like!"

Sometimes a "wild" handbag is chosen because it suggests a certain defiance, readiness to party, or departure from the status quo. One newly divorced woman purchased a vivid yellow, black polka-dotted Manolo Blahnik handbag and matching high-heeled sandals to wear as she embarked on her new life as a single woman. Says she: "I wore this wild bag and shoes for my coming out party after my divorce. (Divorce should not be celebrated but you shouldn't feel like a gross

eunuch, either.) I had on black cigarette pants and a tight shirt and this bag—I may have looked like a hooker but it was important to do.

"I think of it as my nervous-breakdown bag. It's so not me. But I bought it as if to say to my ex: *You think I'm so boring and dull. I'll show you! So there!*"

"Natural" or "wild" materials often turn up in bags: seashells, coconuts, leopard skin, python, crocodile, tortoise, lizard, ostrich feathers, fur, and much more. Sometimes these contribute to a fun mood, as when they are interpreted in unexpected colors: lime green fur, for example, or lavender lizard. Other times bags depict natural themes in a purely whimsical way, such as a straw basket bag, on whose lid perches an idyllic grasshopper, or a tote covered in grass-green Astroturf. Often these bags are meant to be cheerful or whimsical, but they occasionally have a sober subtext as they exhort passersby to remember "endangered Cuban crocodiles" or to "save the elephants."

Whatever the degree of the humor—sophisticated wit or high-spirited hilarity—on one point everyone agrees. It takes a certain sort of attitude to carry a purse that's also a vase, a crab trap, a baseball, a bunny, or some other fanciful object. Says Ann Apple, "When I see someone with a really unusual purse, I think this must be a fun, self-confident, interesting person. It takes confidence to pull off carrying a truly unusual purse!"

*Artist Laura Harris of Florida fabricated this witty "hand" bag around 1980. Made of pink satin and black lace, the bag shows all five fingers of a female's left hand. The fingernails appear to have been "lacquered" red, and the ring finger—third finger, left hand—even boasts a ring.*

The kind of purse you carry makes a statement and sets your mood for the rest of the day. My mother-in-law lived into her nineties and owned many whimsical and fun purses. One was a picnic basket festooned with four little birds and lined in the most vivid aqua. She had an aqua dress to match. So when she chose that dress and matching purse you can imagine how she felt for the day!

—Janie Colwell
Grandmother

*Four bluebirds chatter amongst themselves atop this vintage, decoupaged picnic basket that its owner once used as a summer purse. The aqua lining inside still looks bright and new.*

# ALL THE NAMES I KNOW FROM NURSE

## *Gardener's garters, shepherd's purse*

### BACHELOR BUTTON, LADY'S SMOCK

## AND THE LADY HOLLYHOCK

### FAIRY PLACES, FAIRY THINGS.

—from "The Flowers"
by Robert Louis Stevenson (1850–1894)
Scottish author

*Five whimsical Floralina doll purses by artist Constance Muller of California, line up in a fetching row. Each handmade doll has a hand-painted face, bendable arms, and a full skirt that conceals a small secret compartment where the wearer can stash "tiny treasures, lipsticks, or mad money."*

My Judith Leiber elephant
goes with me
to Republican functions.

—Anonymous

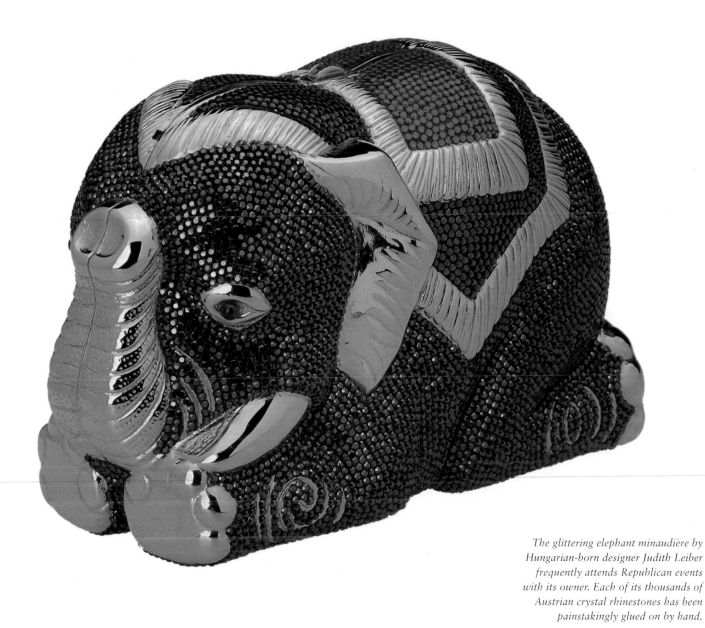

*The glittering elephant minaudière by Hungarian-born designer Judith Leiber frequently attends Republican events with its owner. Each of its thousands of Austrian crystal rhinestones has been painstakingly glued on by hand.*

# Look to the blowing rose about us—Lo,

Laughing, she says, into the world I blow

*At once the silken tassel of my Purse*

Tear, and its Treasure on the Garden Throw.

—from Rubáiyát of Omar Khayyám
by Edward Fitzgerald (1809–1883)
British writer

*Made especially to be sold at a fundraiser benefiting the Center for Women in Charleston, South Carolina, this simple black fabric evening bag has been embellished with genuine ivory piano keys salvaged from a piano and topped with a ruff of sexy black feathers. Designer Linda Plunkett named it "Tickling the Ivories."*

# A WOMAN IN HER LIFETIME WILL SPEND FAR MORE HOURS *hugging a handbag* THAN A MAN.

—Ellen Rachlin
American poet

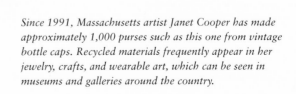

*Since 1991, Massachusetts artist Janet Cooper has made approximately 1,000 purses such as this one from vintage bottle caps. Recycled materials frequently appear in her jewelry, crafts, and wearable art, which can be seen in museums and galleries around the country.*

*"Birthday Cake," "Sunnyside Up," and "Cheesecake" are by Deborah Moissinac/Crysallis. They are one-of-a-kind bags made expressly by the designer to be worn on her own birthday and other special occasions.*

I feel like I am reverting to my childhood when I carry my *Wizard of Oz* lunchbox as a purse. Every year, it was so exciting to pick out a new one. My first was a tartan plaid. My second, a shiny black plastic Barbie with a metal closure that turned, not a latch. Everything fit inside so neatly and compactly. And if you needed a place to sit, you could sit on the lunch box.

—Ann Douglas
Kindergarten teacher

# A HANDBAG IS *fashion's cherry* ON THE SUNDAE.

—Tyler Scott
American writer, contributor to *Skirt!* magazine

*Three marine animals—a seal, a penguin, and a polar bear—appear to drift on an ice floe in this photograph. Synonymous with beauty, quality, and superior workmanship, Leibers such as these are sought by private collectors and museums alike.*

Miss Lucy had a baby.
His name was Tiny Tim.
She put him in the bathtub
To see if he could swim.
He drank up all the water.
He ate up all the soap.

He tried to eat the bathtub
But it wouldn't go down his throat.
Miss Lucy called the doctor.
Miss Lucy called the nurse.
Miss Lucy called the lady
With the alligator purse.

—Children's jump rope rhyme

*These plush animal bags, "Poodle Purse" and "Ollie Terrier Bag," are just two of the many whimsical designs by the North American Bear Company.*

FREUD BELIEVED THAT

HOLLOW RECEPTACLES LIKE PURSES

SYMBOLIZED THE VAGINA . . .

BUT TO PARAPHRASE ANOTHER

OF HIS ALLEGED THOUGHTS,

*a purse is sometimes just a purse*

IN MUCH THE SAME WAY THAT

A CIGAR IS SOMETIMES JUST A CIGAR.

—Sally W. Smith, M.D.
Psychiatrist

*Folded paper-and-cellophane cigarette packs are the design elements of this unusual pair of handbags, which were acquired in the late 1980s and are thought to be examples of prison art.*

# Mystery, Magic, Metaphor, Message

**Women have been** linked with mystery containers—boxes, vials, baskets, bags—ever since Pandora was unable to resist opening the mythic box that contained both pestilence and hope.

The mystery container has been present throughout Western culture, manifesting itself in everything from Little Red Riding Hood's basket, which she carried on her spooky walk through the woods, to the television game show "Let's Make a Deal," in which the host, Monty Hall, had female contestants burrowing frantically through their bags for screwdrivers, flashlights, eggbeaters, and can openers, for which he rewarded them with wads of cash.

Of the two sexes, females are by far the more mysterious. We can nourish with our own milk, heal small wounds, wipe away tears, and generally serve as a fecund resource for whatever ails those around us, capable of pulling out all sorts of magical substances from pockets, folds in garments, and our magical bags.

In all of literature, the most magical of bags belongs, hands down, to the famous nanny Mary Poppins in the 1934 children's novel of the same name by P. L. Travers. Mary Poppins arrives at the Banks household at Number Seventeen Cherry-Tree Lane, blowing in on a gust of the East Wind and carrying an umbrella and carpetbag.

The Banks children, Jane and Michael, are completely mystified by this odd person and her large bag.

"What a funny bag," he said, pinching it with his fingers.

"Carpet," said Mary Poppins, putting her key in the lock.

"To carry carpets in, you mean?"

"No. Made of."

"Oh," said Michael. "I see." But he didn't—quite.

By this time the bag was open, and Jane and Michael were more than surprised to find it was completely empty.

"Why," said Jane, "there's nothing in it!"

"What do you mean—nothing?" demanded Mary Poppins, drawing herself up and looking as though she had been insulted. "Nothing in it, did you say?"

*Leaves, berries, mosses, and twigs (although they are faux) make a natural statement in this handbag, made by artist Kelly Chambers.*

And with that she took out from the empty bag a starched white apron and tied it round her waist. Next she unpacked a large cake of Sunlight Soap, a toothbrush, a packet of hairpins, a bottle of scent, a small folding armchair and a box of throat lozenges.

A few minutes later, she pulls out yet more impossible objects from the "empty" carpet bag: "seven flannel nightgowns, four cotton ones, a pair of boots, a set of dominoes, two bathing caps, and a postcard album. Last of all came a folding camp-bedstead with blankets and eiderdown complete . . ."

The children are completely spellbound. The little boy cries to Mary Poppins, ". . . you'll never leave us, will you?"

Mary Poppins is the female equivalent of a *magus*, or magician, and her bag is the bottomless hat out of which endless scarves, rabbits, and anything else may come, to the utter enchantment of children.

The handbag may be said to speak a magical language, and that language is metaphor.

It is a bosom or organ, a tender anatomical part.

It is a brain, an intelligence that works when the memory doesn't.

It is a third eye, a watchful defender.

It is a uterus, from which spring the progeny of necessity and invention.

It is a subconscious, a seat of hidden impulses and conflicts.

It is a haven, a refuge into which one can retreat.

It is a nest, fashioned out of the twigs and bits and flotsam one needs to nourish a life.

It is the most private of rooms, a sanctum sanctorum.

It is even a church, temple, or soul.

Many handbags contain soulful objects: a prayer book, rosary, Star of David, religious medal, or sacred crystal. Some of these are carried to or from a place of worship in the handbag; others are pulled out or handled on a city bus, park bench, or waiting room, whenever or wherever a woman wants to have a moment of meditation, contemplation, or prayer.

Sometimes, the fetishes carried within the bag have more to do with superstition. To wit: rabbit's feet, four-leaf clovers, lucky-seven charms, even the occasional voodoo doll!

So mysterious and potent are handbags that they may be said to possess *us* as much as we possess them. Their hold on us is twofold.

*These two liquid metallic bags with collage designs are from Brazilian Carlos Falchi's 2001 spring collection. The small blue clutch has patches of genuine python. The large electric pink hobo bag also features real snakeskin undulating in a lively, wavelike rhythm across the front.*

First, our dependence on them is quite literal and real. And second, their symbolism and metaphysics are obvious, compelling, even near-mystical. And the relationship between handbag and owner is wildly unbalanced. Certainly we need our handbags more than they need us; indeed, they don't need us at all.

Could it even be that handbags have a secret life, a universe parallel to our own where all sorts of inexplicable things are being—or not being—worked out: conspiracies, imbroglios, subplots? Could this explain what happens to lost objects? Could a handbag even be a final resting place for all those identities we shed over the years, after we've outgrown them?

> "My ex-husband gave me a beautiful Italian evening bag which I soon realized was a metaphor for our marriage. Both the bag and the marriage were all about form without function. The purse looked nice on the outside but its interior was shallow and dysfunctional. It was too sleek and slim to hold any contents. Shortly after he gave it to me, I knew our marriage wouldn't last."
>
> —J.R.
> Restaurant critic

Handbags often send messages, either to the owners or about the owners. I am playful. I am serious. I mean business. I am bohemian. I am crazy. I am wealthy. I am establishment. I am anti-establishment. I am artistic. I am feminine. I want you to notice me. A number of women decode other women by scrutinizing their bags. Sometimes you *can* judge a book by its cover!

Observes Ellen Levine, editor of *Good Housekeeping* magazine: "Handbags are a real indulgence and reward because a busy woman does not have to try them on: they always fit. But I have noticed that one way to tell the difference between a woman with a time-consuming job and a woman with a little bit more time to herself is her handbag. If the handbag gets changed every day and the shoes match, the chances are she's got time off! No one I know has the hours in her days to really coordinate their accessories."

Athene Jordan, a South Carolina artist, believes that the degree to which a woman is ditzy is in inverse proportion to the size of her purse. "Sometimes," she says, "purse size can give away how efficient a person is, or how big of an airhead, as in *I just had to have this little purse to match my lipstick and outfit*. Recently one of these women asked me for a pen because she didn't have one in her pocketbook. When I pulled out a Bic, she said, 'A Bic? I always use a Mount Blanc.' Get a life, honey!"

Sometimes the handbag delivers a succinct message to the wearer, in the form of a "lesson" she never forgets. Victoria Reggio, a writer who was mugged, clung to her handbag as her attacker pulled her hair and dragged her to the ground.

"As soon as I let go, he grabbed the bag and ran . . . I got a new bag, and as the compartments in my life mended and filled, I never forgot the lesson I learned the night of my mugging," recounts Victoria. *"Let go!"*

Another woman, Jerri Chaplin, a poetry therapist, also received an important message through the medium of a handbag. Her mother died recently and Jerri went through her things. "I discovered a beautiful white leather Prada handbag with the sale tag still on it. It had been a seven hundred dollar bag that she bought for $299. Never used, it was like receiving a message from my mother after she was gone: 'Don't save whatever it is you are saving—the perfume or the silver in the drawer—for a special future time. Use it *now*!'"

Finally, the bag is capable of delivering a direct sexual message. In *The Language of Clothes,* Alison Lurie observes that the handbag is "the most universally recognized sexual indicator in women." She theorizes that the term *old bag* "may be subliminally responsible for the female readiness to discard even a slightly worn purse. As a result, secondhand shops are full of old bags, often expensive leather ones, which, though perfectly functional and in good condition, have been rejected by their owners."

Lurie further states "the bag conveys erotic information, if only in the eyes of the beholder. According to my male informants, a tightly snapped, zipped, and buckled purse suggests a woman who guards her physical and emotional privacy closely, one whom it will be difficult to get to know in either the common or the Biblical sense. An open-topped tote bag suggests an open, trusting nature: someone who is emotionally and sexually more accessible."

*The mixed bright python collage clutch was designed by Carlos Falchi in the late 1970s. The smaller envelope-style bag from the 1980s depicts a pair of flamenco dancers and is made from a mixture of leather and snakeskin.*

Queen Elizabeth (I) had a girdle-bag, or pouch, containing miniature editions of Seneca, verses by Petrarch, writing materials, sweets, and herbal remedies, which she gave to her privy counselors to save them from the horrors of Tudor medicine.

—from an essay that appeared in *The Spectator*
by Paul Johnson

I don't want to wear a dress or pocketbook so outstanding or special that it's all people want to talk about all night. My daughter, Gregg, once deliberated over buying a stunning pink evening gown with a plunging neckline and I said, "Are you sure you want to deal with that dress?" She said, "Mom, I think I can handle it," and indeed people talked to her about it all night long.

I think it's boring to spend a night having six people ask you, "Where did you buy that?" If you talk about something you are wearing the other person doesn't get to talk and you don't get to listen and learn.

You might be with a real person, a spiritual person, who has fascinating stories. You would miss this person altogether because your attention was focused on your pocketbook.

—Nancy Smythe
American poet and grandmother

*These two grosgrain fabric bags are by Merrilee. The red bag on the left features a cheerful circular handle and plump black pompoms. The holiday bag on the right sports a Christmas tree decorated with miniature Christmas ornaments and beads, finished with a sparkly star on top.*

# IN SUM, THE PURSE IS A PERFECT UNKNOWN, AN UNRECOGNIZED INTRIGUER. IT IS AN INEXHAUSTIBLE FOUNT OF MYSTERIES AND METAPHORS. IT IS THE MODERN TRANSCRIPTION OF THE CLASSICAL PANDORA'S BOX: A PLACE FOR IRREPRESSIBLE CURIOSITY, FOR SECRETS NEVER UNVEILED, AND INSIDIOUS PENALTIES.

—from "The Bag as Destiny"
by Mariuccia Casadio
an essay from the book *In the Bag*,
edited by Samuele Mazza

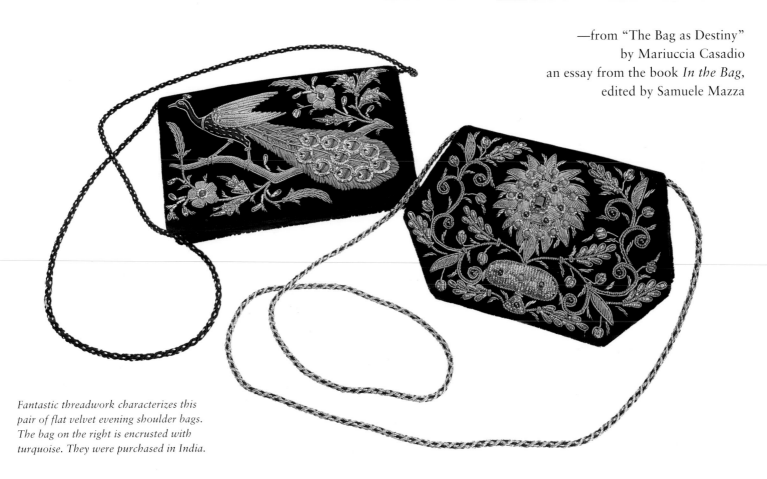

*Fantastic threadwork characterizes this pair of flat velvet evening shoulder bags. The bag on the right is encrusted with turquoise. They were purchased in India.*

MYSTERY, MAGIC, METAPHOR, MESSAGE 103

THE PURSE IS A MYSTERY OBJECT WHICH MEN APPROACH MUCH AS THEY APPROACH A WOMAN FOR INTIMACY . . . WHICH IS TO SAY, *with fear and vulnerability.* SHE IS NOT GOING TO LET HIM IN EASILY.

—Sally W. Smith, M.D.
Psychiatrist

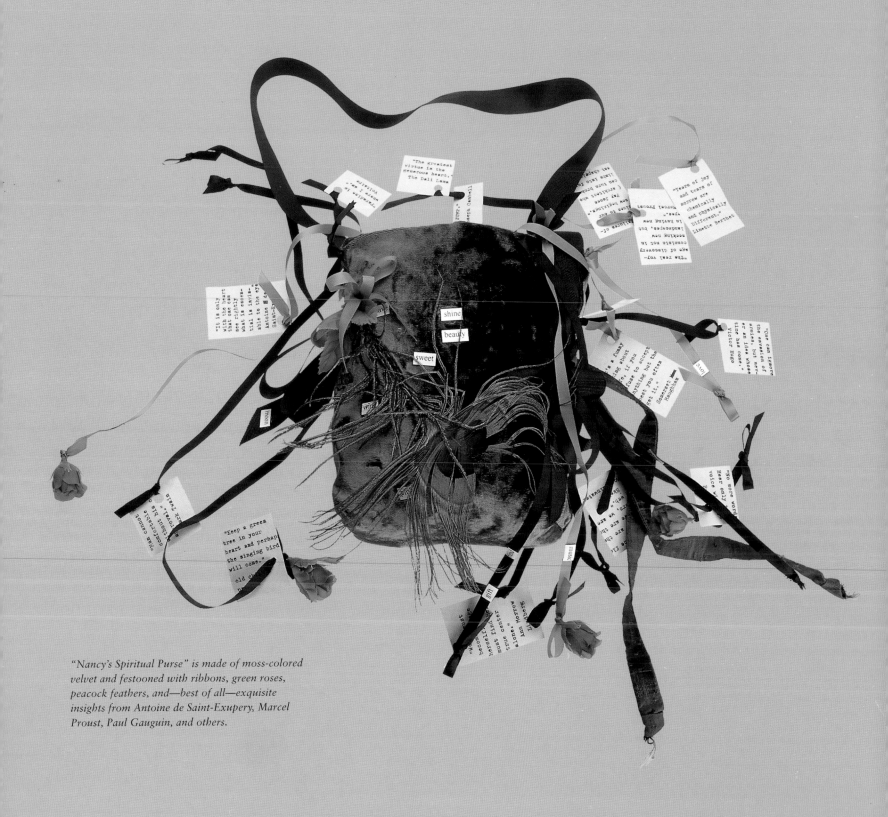

"Nancy's Spiritual Purse" is made of moss-colored velvet and festooned with ribbons, green roses, peacock feathers, and—best of all—exquisite insights from Antoine de Saint-Exupery, Marcel Proust, Paul Gauguin, and others.

# Dreams & Desires

*Handbags* regularly occupy women's dreams—both daydreams and night dreams. By day, they are objects of intense desire, whether for their extrinsic value or for their magical properties. By night, they haunt women's dreams as a symbol of the self, energy, identity, or autonomy.

In the course of speaking to women about their handbags, I sometimes became aware of an ardor so intense for certain bags that it bordered on *lust*. A woman may become, for any number of reasons, fixated upon obtaining a prized handbag. She's as willing, strategic, cunning, and patient as any soldier to claim it in victory! Sometimes she must somehow manipulate the household budget; other times she must outwit or out-wait her relatives.

Strong sentiment may motivate her. Several granddaughters described to me their stratagems for snagging the bags of their deceased grandmothers. "Her handbags were the only things I wanted," says one who sat quietly while other relatives picked through the grandmother's more outwardly valuable belongings. "I waited until they had chosen and then I took her wonderful plastic handbags."

Sometimes a dream bag is an obsession because it is a high-status or rare item. Many desire it. Few can have it. There's a nine-month wait list. It has a haughty provenance. It's a collector's item. It took twenty hours to make. Twelve artisans worked on it. Two thousand, five hundred stitches were put in by hand. The bag was named for, and inspired by, actress Jane Birkin (Hermès) or Catherine Deneuve (Fendi). The singer Madonna or supermodel Kate Moss was pictured carrying one in *Vogue* or at a Hollywood event. The handbag will accrue in value. Only two hundred of them were ever made. This is all the stuff of obsession, the stuff that fuels daydreams and causes women to write large checks. (One woman observes dryly: "It's men who have penis envy. Women have *purse envy*.")

Then there is the purely fanciful dream purse, which exists only in the imagination. The fact that it doesn't exist and never will only adds to its allure as an object of fantasy. Linda Fantuzzo is an artist whose dream purse is a sculpture with strong aesthetic appeal. "If weight were not an issue," muses Linda, "I'd carry a cast bronze purse or perhaps one fashioned from sheets of lead. It's the shape and patina of a bag that interests me."

The elusive search for perfection—the utopian handbag, ingenious solver of problems and perfect sidekick—is a frequent refrain. Says Nikki Hardin, editor of *Skirt!* magazine: "I am fifty-seven years old and still searching for the perfect purse. I think it lives in a tiny shop off a winding side street in Rome. It is made of weathered caramel leather, as capacious as an old Pony Express bag yet small. It shrinks and expands to fit my needs and magically organizes my life. Perhaps we will meet in another lifetime."

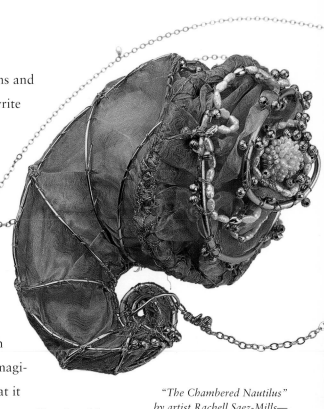

*"The Chambered Nautilus" by artist Rachell Saez-Mills—constructed of fabric and wire and attached to a delicate chain—is as much an exquisite* objet d'art *as it is a functional evening handbag.*

Phyllis Theroux is a writer in Ashland, Virginia, whose ideal purse has been engineered by a dreamer's imagination: "Here's my invention for the Perfect Purse. It lights up, like the inside of a refrigerator, when you open it. There are enough dividers, pockets, and zippered compartments for keys, lipstick, rain poncho, Weight Watchers points counter, Mace, wire cutters, and aspirin to thin your blood in the event of a heart attack. You can plug it into a wall outlet and get your e-mail, fill it with water (unplug first) and wash your laundry in it. With the Perfect Purse you can be anywhere and be secure, knowing that you are fully prepared for any emergency—except an earthquake. For that you need another invention I am working on—a giant sling shot that will hurl you into the air until the earthquake's over."

The handbags of nocturnal dreams are no less insistent in their claim upon our attention. Handbags are standard items—as are clocks, keys, cars, and so forth—in dream

This Chanel handbag combines the whimsy of a charm bracelet with the sophisticated elegance of a fine leather, quilted bag.

imagery. *The Handbook Of Dream Analysis* by Emil A. Gutheil, M.D., drawing on the work of Sigmund Freud, the Austrian founder of psychoanalysis and pioneer in the interpretation of dreams, offers the following list of female symbols in dreams: "bag, pocket, wound, nest, cavern, ring, target, muff, front door, room, window, pot, box, cage, stove, pool of water, lake, boat, drawer, and other similar things."

The loss of one's handbag is perhaps the most common of dream liefmotifs. Writes Linda Leonard in her well-known book on female psychology, *The Wounded Woman:* "One dream theme is the loss of one's pocketbook, with all one's identity cards and money. For example, one woman dreamt her man friend had left her, and when she tried to go home, she realized she had no money. The only means of transportation she could take was a school bus for children. . . . [This] dream motif reveal[s] the danger of losing one's own source of energy and identity [symbolized by the loss of money and pocketbook]. . . ."

One woman writer has had many handbag dreams, which have all but disappeared as she has shed some emotional baggage. Interestingly, she dislikes handbags in her waking life, considers them a "necessary evil," and is happiest "when I can stick a key and a twenty-dollar bill in my pocket and do without the ——book altogether."

She observes: "In my dreams, handbags represent my identity, sometimes specific aspects of it. For a number of years, when I was first starting to try to figure myself out, I would find it; other times it remained lost. I always felt anxious about these dreams and have taken pleasure recently in realizing that I rarely, if ever, have these dreams anymore.

I hope this means I have made some progress in 'finding my bag' in my waking hours and no longer have to spend all night trying to find it."

About the same time that Freud was doing his groundbreaking work, Dr. Carl Jung, the great Swiss psychologist, was also doing seminal work in dream interpretation. It was he who introduced the idea of the "collective unconscious." By that he meant the shared part of the human psyche, common to all humanity throughout the ages, which contains and transmits universal psychic imagery, archetypes, and symbols. Surely handbags and purses—having, as their antecedents, bags, boxes, casks, and other containers familiar to ancients in all cultures—exist in the collective unconscious.

Dr. Sally W. Smith says, "On the Jungian side, there is the idea of the female connection to the collective unconscious. Every woman has the tie or connection to this stream, which flows under us as humans.

The purse may symbolize our female version of the collective unconscious: think of the darkness of the purse, the way it is closed up, and the way the universality of its contents (such as tampons and lipstick) unites us. It's as if our shadow selves, our underworld, are hanging together off our shoulders as we push our carts through the supermarket."

*The whimsical "Grasshopper on Basket" by Deborah Moissinac/Crysallis evokes an idyllic summer day. It has a snug-fitting lid and simple cord handle.*

# MY SEARCH FOR THE IDEAL GOES ON. I HAVE A FEELING IT WILL END ONLY WHEN THEY CART ME OFF TO A NURSING HOME, JAIL, OR WHEREVER I WON'T NEED A HANDBAG, MUCH LESS ITS CONTENTS.

—Wendy Sizer
American writer

*"Bucket of Roses," made in 1999, is MooRoo's signature handbag. Finest silk roses are clustered atop a black satin, bucket-shaped bag with a short, curved handle.*

It was a black evening bag sequined with salt, open-mouthed under a rusted marcasite clasp, revealing a black moiré silk lining stained by seawater; a relic stranded in the wrack of tarry pebbles and tufts of blue and orange nylon string like garish sea anemones, crab shells and lobster legs, plastic detritus, oily feathers, condoms and rubbery weed and clouded gloss, the dry white sponges of whelk egg cases, and a brittle black-horned mermaid's purse. The image, the wreckage of a dream beached on the morning, would not float away; as empty as an open shell, the black bivalve emitted a silent howl of despair; clouds passed through its mirror.

—from *Dreams of Dead Women's Handbags*
by Shena Mackay
British writer

*Iridescent pearls and sequins enliven this basic black vintage clutch and give it a three-dimensional look. Its fabric wristband handle is concealed.*

# WE ARE SUCH STUFF AS
# DREAMS ARE MADE ON.

—from *The Tempest*
by William Shakespeare (1564–1616)
English playwright and poet

*Jazzy and kicky, this orange-feathered handbag has a short beaded strap. It is new from Wooden Ships.*

# Let us all have one purse.

## *(Marsupium unum sit omnium nostrum.)*

—Proverbs, 1:14.

*This Louis Vuitton has a drawstring closure
and exceptionally roomy interior. Vuitton
founded his eponymous shop in Paris in 1854.*

[the purse is]

# The master-organ,

## soul's seat,

### and true pineal gland

## of the body social.

—from *Sartor Resartus*
by Thomas Carlyle (1795–1881)
Scottish historian, critic, and sociological writer

A pair of swans floats lazily in the foreground of this antique, glass-beaded purse. "Scenic" purses such as this one often depict swans, castles, lakes, cottages, gardens, and other pastoral, romantic motifs.

This trio of fur bags includes two "real" and one "faux." At top is "Lara" by MooRoo, trimmed in dyed fox. The bag at right is made of genuine leopard, allegedly shot on safari by the owner's husband's grandmother in the 1930s. The largest of the three is a fabulous fake made by Gauchita in 2002.

# MY PURSE,
## MY PERSON,
### *my extremest means*
### LIE ALL UNLOCKED TO YOUR OCCASIONS.

—from *The Merchant of Venice*
by William Shakespeare (1564–1616)
English playwright and poet

# Responsibility & Freedom

*The handbag* represents responsibilities, and although women are "freer" now than ever before, their duties have multiplied. A typical woman at the beginning of the millennium has children *and* a job, a house *and* an office. And if she is one of the approximately 40 million baby boomer women, a member of the so-called "sandwich generation," she may also have her parents to care for, plus the responsibility of the laundry, cleaning, shopping, gardening, running errands, and a dog or cat. Her overloaded bag may well represent an overloaded individual, bulging as it does with dry cleaner tickets, coupons, a baby rattle, calculator, spillover office work, and the PTA schedule.

Says Cada McCoy, who owns a small, exquisite collection of heirloom purses: "I almost resent my purse. I am attracted to them, and have a closet full of them. But I am tied to my purse, which represents everything I am responsible for: my bank account, my keys. I don't like it!"

Athene Jordan—a busy wife, mother, and artist—perceives the overstuffed handbag as a reflection of the myriad roles every woman fills, and also of our talents and versatility. After all, what man has ever consummated a business deal over the cell phone while coaching his daughter's softball game and feeding an infant a bottle at the same time? "Men," she observes, "don't multitask. We women multitask like crazy. We're more efficient because we have to be. To do that, we need all our gadgets and toys and tricks with us."

Many handbags are chosen with duty and efficiency in mind. The first criterion is size. "I like large bags," says one woman. "Small bags only worked in the days when all one cared about was having a package of cigarettes and a lighter or matches." (Another said, "If it's not big enough for a book or a journal, then it's not big enough.") It is safe to surmise that, as a general rule, the larger the bag, the more numerous the duties. Commodious handbags may pack an iPod, Elph, spandex running shorts, extra diaper, carton of juice, overdue library books and videos, and a stethoscope—a Babel of articles that points to the complexity of a woman's roles. And we don't even want to *think* about women who carry two or three bags, though goodness knows many of those, burdened like pack animals, may be sighted on the urban or suburban landscape as they dash from minivan to daycare to office.

With duty and utility in mind, a woman may choose a purse that is black (won't show dirt), made of nylon (easy to wash off), and full of nooks and crannies (the better to organize her fragmented, compartmentalized life). It may have a hard surface, like a desk, for writing, and contain enough paraphernalia that one may work on a novel, prepare a brief, or figure taxes virtually anywhere, anytime. Says Leila

*This bold yellow and orange zippered leather handbag is new from Christian Livingston. Similar in feel to a bowling bag, it has a playful, youthful quality.*

Hadley Luce: "Without a handbag and supplies of pens and paper, I feel I'm without a desk, without a magic helper to write *aides memoires* about people and things and ideas and thoughts and must-do notes. (When traveling in Africa or Asia, I always carry extra magic markers or ballpoint pens to give to school-age children who sometimes can't go to school if they don't have a pen. Magic markers are *the* present for children, not candies. That actually is true anywhere in the world.)"

Some women resent the responsibilities the purse represents; others resent the purses themselves. Heavy, clumsy, clunky, full of stuff we have to do . . . as opposed to what we want to do. Virginia Parker of Atlanta, Georgia, a senior copywriter for a major corporation and mother of three, comments, "A purse is as essential as family—and as much a burden as it is a support. You have to track it like a toddler. It's too big to pick up, but you can't safely put it down."

Some women associate certain handbags with their hard-won freedom and other bags—the prim and proper variety—with the constraints they worked so hard to overthrow. Writes Anne Rivers Siddons, the novelist, who came of age in the pre-civil rights South:

"When I was a child in Fairburn, Georgia, twenty miles and one hundred years south of Atlanta, a purse was

*Designed by Mary Frances Shaffer of Mary Frances Accessories, "Dog Show" is from her Motif collection. Mary Frances's vividly-colored, richly-ornamented handbags are made by skilled artisans and possess an exotic, jewel-like quality.*

the ultimate symbol of respectable ladyhood. These objects were uncompromisingly four square and impregnable, made of black or navy blue leather (for Sunday) and leatherette (for everyday). They hung like a dead cat from the hand of the wearer, and were never called anything but pocketbooks. I have spent my life avoiding them.

"Since the first purse I can remember, a shiny red Scottie dog hanging from a gold chain, I have loved shoulder bags and have rarely owned any other kind. To do so seems like giving up something I value, giving in to something I don't. I love the swing-and-dash of shoulder bags, the cheerful slap against the hip, the sheer in-your-face freedom. To me, the greatest era in the history of pursedom was the Sixties, when quilted leather purses swung on double gold chains from every other female shoulder in America. It is a pursely time warp I am still happily stuck in. If I ever acquire a pocketbook, I am afraid I will, finally, have to grow up."

Many women report using their entire car as a purse, especially when they want to "travel light" while shopping. The BMW key and American Express card go into a pocket, the handbag is locked inside a trunk, and a woman is ready to take on the mall! Sonya Livingston's bags, some stored in her car, call to mind the nesting Russian dolls, the *matryoshka*, with each purse concealed within a slightly larger one, her car being the biggest "purse" of all.

"I am," avows Sonya, "a bag lady, a true pocketbook aficionada. There are about eighteen bags in my car right now. I have one thousand black bags. And inside my black work purse there are several smaller purses, and inside of one of those a tiny black Chanel. . . ."

Amy Fine Collins lives in New York City where women primarily use public transportation, and therefore necessarily have to carry more possessions with them. Notes Amy: "A purse is to a woman what a car is to a man. In cities where there is a highly evolved car culture, there is less need for a purse. Most of the bulky things a Manhattanite might throw into her bag—a book, an extra pair of stockings, a pack of cigarettes—an L.A. woman would simply leave in her car."

Hands free. Calendars clear. Duties magically lifted. The fantasy is appealing, and yet would we really want to be without some of those tasks which tie us to loved ones, to community, to the world of work and the larger universe of people? Would we really want to be "bagless?" I once spent two special weeks writing at an artists' colony where there were no telephones, no chores, nothing to do but work, think, and be solitary. Even lunch simply "materialized" at each artist's studio door every day. For months I could hardly wait to get away from home and obligations, but once in the artist's colony I made an important discovery: I *missed* my life which was so wonderfully cluttered with people, responsibilities, "bags," "baggage," and the ties that bind.

*Christian Livingston recently created this double-handled, basket-like straw summer purse. Its design of flowers and leaves evokes a summer garden in full bloom.*

When it comes to balancing freedom and responsibility, I think most females are like Frederica Mathewes-Green of Maryland, a writer for the Internet publication Beliefnet, who left her pocketbook atop the car one night at a gas station and didn't realize it until arriving at her mother-in-law's house forty-five minutes later.

"It was too dark to search then, but all night I fretted. Had it fallen off right in the gas station lot, and was someone even now using my Visa card to order a vintage Corvette? Was some fan using the cell phone to leave long messages on Ricky Martin's answering machine?

"We set the alarm for an hour before sunrise and soon were back in the car, gliding along and scanning the other side of the highway.

"And there it was. A quick U-turn and we were upon it. Picture a black leather pocketbook, about the size of a small shoebox, run over. Its long braided strap, snapped, tailed out in a curl on the gray pavement.

"We parked and walked up for a closer look. The purse was still zipped, but had been popped open and exploded. Everything was smashed. The little blue-backed mirror was in fragments, reflecting the pearly sky, and the red and blue ballpoint pens and a pink nail file were scattered around like confetti. The crushed highlighter splayed its yellow fibers, fanned out into a brush. The fuchsia lipstick was only bent, but the red one was good and smashed, and lumps and streaks of red were scribbled throughout the scene.

"It was strangely festive. Then I came on the cell phone. This was best of all. It had been a large, clunky old phone, and it made an impressive spill that ran 20 feet or more. It was kind of exhilarating.

"I walked along in the chill. As I got to the end of the broken phone trail, I looked up the road toward the pale pink horizon. For one crazy moment, I thought I could just go on walking.

"Then I thought a little more. I *could* just go on walking, and in a few hours all I'd get to would be Ravenel. I had been through Ravenel many times, and I didn't think it would be improved by walking.

*This small, flat bag by Nila has a cord handle, toggle clasp, and a floral pattern so simple that it verges upon abstraction. Bags like this one are especially loved by travelers because they take up no room in a suitcase.*

"I kept thinking about why the sight of an exploded pocketbook would be so gratifying. It seemed a sudden opportunity to be free from all these nattering things that pin us down, that incessantly whine of their importance. A pocketbook is literal weight, and you must guard it closely or encounter catastrophe.

"Seeing it so run over, so irrelevant and powerless, gave me a strange, momentary rush of freedom. It was a timid taste of what some more daring individuals must feel when they plunge into exhilarating, forbidden adventures and cast off propriety.

"But even for them, there must be a wan morning-after. For me, all my freedom deflated as I pictured myself trudging through Ravenel.

"In the car, I started to make a list of things to replace. Perhaps this time I'd go for a red wallet instead of a black one. I'd need to shop for a new cell phone, too, one of those tiny ones. There would be a lot of small, complicated things to gather as I rebuilt that nest of security, and it would be interesting to make decisions. This was going to be fun."

Ultimately, the image of a woman with a bag calls to mind the archetype of the seeker, the traveler. In a very real sense, we are all cosmic voyagers and visitors, moving ever forward—handbag in hand—on the roads of our individual destinies. With the objects, trifles, talismans, and necessities we've assembled in our bags, we are poised for life's adventures as our unique feminine stories continue to unfold.

I schlep totes now that I work in the corporate world. My tote is a cave that contains the map to my life—what I'm currently interested in, responsible for, and creating. I can't wait to be free of it.

—Virginia Parker
Senior copywriter

Florida, made this "Island Tote," which was inspired by the tropics. The cotton print bag has natural vachetta handles and depicts two different, painterly scenes of the Caribbean on its front and back.

# A LIGHT PURSE
## MAKES A HEAVY HEART.

—from *Emblemes and Epigrames*, 1600
by Francis Thynne (1545(?)–1608)
British writer

*"Tropical Bamboo" by designer Lindsay Russell/Etoile is made of fabric evocative of the jungle with its palm trees and banana leaves. This casual summer bag is attached to double bamboo handles and finished with a jaunty red plastic fringe.*

# A heavy purse
## *makes a light heart.*

—from "The New Inne"
by Ben Jonson (1572(?)–1637)
English dramatist and poet

*Vibrant hues of silk dupioni dramatize these classically elegant bags by Gianna Costas/San Juan. The bags close with black grosgrain ribbon ties.*

# Selected Readings

Allen, Carmel. *The Handbag: To Have and to Hold*. London: Carlton Books Limited, 1999.

Dooner, Kate. *A Century of Handbags*. Atglen, Pa.: Schiffer Publishing, Ltd., 1993.

Ettinger, Roseann. *Handbags*. West Chester, Pa.: Schiffer Publishing, Ltd., 1991.

———. *Handbags*, 3rd ed. Atglen, Pa.: Schiffer Publishing Ltd., 1999.

Foster, Vanda. *Bags and Purses*. London: B.T. Batsford, Ltd., 1982.

Lurie, Alison, *The Language of Clothes*. New York: Owl Books, 2000.

Mazza, Samuele, ed. *In the Bag*. San Francisco: Chronicle Books, 1997.

Schwartz, Lynell K. *Vintage Purses at their Best*. Atglen, Pa.: Schiffer Publishing, Ltd., 1995.

Steele, Valerie, and Laird Borrelli. *Handbags: A Lexicon of Style*. New York City: Rizzoli International Publications, Inc., 1999.

Wilcox, Claire. *A Century of Bags*. Edison, N.J.: Chartwell Books, 1997.

———. *Bags*. London: V & A Publications, 1999.

# Photography Credits

Photographs © Jack Alterman

We would like to acknowledge the following collectors and suppliers who so generously loaned us the bags photographed in *Handbags*:

Collection of Ann Apple: p. 122

Collection of Marti Atkins: p. 62

Collection of Kiara Balish: p. 23

Collection of Elizabeth Boggs: p. 22

Collection of Tippy Stern Brickman: pp. 37, 113

Courtesy of Carlos Falchi: pp. 28, 74, 100

© Chanel: pp. 36, 41, 108

Courtesy Christian Livingston: pp. 119, 121

Collection of Jeane Haskins Colwell: pp. 81, 84, 111

Collection of Theresa Cox: p. 51

Collection of Harriett Daughtridge: pp. 19 (left and top), 59, 69, 79

Courtesy of Deborah Moissinac/Crysallis: pp. 90, 109

Collection of Mary Douglas: pp. 47, 101

Courtesy of Gianna Costas/San Juan: pp. 38, 76, 125 (right)

Collection of Gretchen Freeman: p. 95

Courtesy of Gauchita: p. 116 (center)

Collection of Gervais Hagerty: p. 89

Collection of Bessie Hanahan: pp. 37 (right), 103

Collection of Dora Appel Handel: pp. 14, 15, 29 (left), 44, 61

Courtesy of Savannah Knoop: p. 20

Collection of Peggy Lewis: p. 88, 102 (left), 107

Courtesy of Lindsay Russell/Etiole: p. 124

Collection of Sonya Livingston: p. 29 (right)

Courtesy of Merrilee: p. 102 (right)

Courtesy of Mary Frances Accessories: pp. 17, 21, 120

Collection of Cada McCoy: pp. 49, 52, 83, 115

Collection of Jane McFadden: p. 116 (right)

Collection of Carol McLaren: p. 55

Courtesy of Sandra L. Mohlmann: pp. 19 (right), 25, 39, 50 (left), 73, 75

Courtesy of MooRoo: pp. 3, 16, 56, 82 (bottom), 116 (left)

Courtesy of Constance Muller: p. 85

"Poodle Purse" and "Ollie Terrier Bag" © North American Bear Co., Inc. All rights reserved.: p. 93

Courtesy of Oroton: pp. 30, 35

Collection of Leslie H. Pelzer, M.D.: p. 67

Courtesy of Norma May Fashion Art Accessories: p. 33

Collection of Carlene Sessions: pp. 82 (top), 87, 92

Collection of Nancy Smythe: p. 105

Collection of Agnes M. Street: p. 125 (center)

Courtesy of Stubbs & Wootton: p. 123

Collection of Laura Szweda: p. 27

Courtesy of Paige Hathaway Thorne: p. 42

Collection of Lori Wyatt: pp. 32, 53, 58, 65, 70

All other handbags are from the author's collection.

Special thanks to Norma May of Norma May International, whose shop at 315 King Street in Charleston, South Carolina, is a phantasmagoria of Fashion Art Accessories (843-577-8884).

# About the Author

**Barbara G. S. Hagerty** is a writer, photographer, and visual essayist who received bachelor's and master's degrees from The Johns Hopkins University. Her writing has appeared in more than twenty-five magazines and newspapers nationwide, including *The Los Angeles Times, Town & Country, The Ladies' Home Journal, Child, Saveur, The Atlanta Journal-Constitution*, and *Travel & Leisure*. Her book, *Purse Universe*—a gallery of photographic portraits of purse owners accompanied by text—was published in 2001 by Crane Hill Publishers. She lives with her husband and four children in South Carolina, where they divide their time between Charleston and rural Edisto Island. She invites readers to visit her website at www.barbarahagerty.com, or to write her directly at bhagerty1@aol.com.